The
SETTLE-CARL
The Middle Route to Scotland

W R Mitchell

Bob Swallow

Published by
Kingfisher Productions
Watershed Mill, Settle, North Yorkshire BD24 9LR
www.railwayvideo.com

Contents

All photographs from the author's collection unless otherwise credited. Every effort has been made to identify the source of each photograph, apologies are extended if the origin of a picture was not correctly credited.

Front cover: **Stanier Jubilee Class No. 45697** Achilles **hauls a northbound freight over Ribblehead on 26th August 1966.** Roy Hobbs

Publisher - Roger Hardingham
Copyright W. R. Mitchell &
Kingfisher Productions
ISBN 978-0-946184-97-2
Printed in England

Overview

The Settle-Carlisle Railway was built on a heroic scale. The work took place in the 1870s during a short, feverish spell of activity at a cost of almost £3½m, more than 50 per cent over the budget figure. Other railway companies having claimed the east and west routes to Scotland, a middle course was "the only possible one that nature has left." Frustrated at working arrangements with the Lancaster-Carlisle, the Midland modified a scheme put forward locally and extended it "over the tops" to Carlisle.

The Settle-Carlisle was the last major railway in the land created, in time-honoured manner, by the muscular efforts of a considerable labour force and a modicum of heavy equipment. It would be written that the line penetrated a region through which nothing but unlimited capital and indomitable energy could have carried it. Vertical steam engines, similar to those used for constructing city sewers, were transported to the heads of projected tunnel shafts. Hundreds of horses hauled wagons on tramways from the new cuttings to where embankments were required. In 1873, a new Burleigh rock drill, introduced to work at Birkett, above Mallerstang, enabled a hole a foot deep to be made in five minutes.

Midland surveyors and engineers made clever use of two north-south valleys, those of Eden and Ribble, and had their abilities stretched to an extreme on the tract of high Pennines that lay between. An engineer compared the Settle-Carlisle with a whale "lying on its belly, with the nose at Settle, its tail at Carlisle, A steep ascent carries us up; a long incline carries us down." The ruling gradient on the Drag from Settle to Aisgill was fixed at 1 in 100. When the work was done, weariness set in among those involved. Work that should have taken four years had dragged on for six and a-half. The Midland Board was desperate for a return on the money spent.

Matthew Kirtley's locomotives, wearing dark green livery, inaugurated the passenger service, drawing Pullman stock that set new standards of luxury in rail travel. Even ordinary coaches, riding on six-wheeled bogies, on all-steel rails, moved with unaccustomed smoothness. Third-class passengers, for long the despised section of the rail-travelling public, occupied upholstered seats when most other companies provided wooden benches.

An ex-LMS Jubilee class on the Settle-Carlisle - a perfect combination. No 45596 Bahamas **hauls 'The Cumbrian Mountain Express' through Mallerstang in the early 1990s.**
Peter Fox

The most famous of them all - the great viaduct at Ribblehead, seen shortly after renovation in 1992. BR

In modern times, the Settle-Carlisle, doomed to closure, was miraculously reprieved. Not so the Hawes branch, which was closed in 1964. The metals were lifted and the track is now grassed over. (Further down the dale the Wensleydale Railway, a private concern, is active and dreams of re-establishing the old link with Garsdale). For 10 years, diesels-only operated on the Settle-Carlisle for British Railways did not want steam locomotives to pass under its precious new electric wires near Carlisle. Then, in 1978, a steam-hauled train returned. Despite atrocious weather – mist and driving snow – a gala atmosphere prevailed around Ribblehead viaduct as hundreds of people gathered to watch its progress. We saw a plume of smoke, a shade denser than the mist, and The Green Arrow appeared, speeding towards the viaduct, being little more than a smudge against the swirling vapour.

It was enough to alleviate in the keenest observers yet another attack of Settle-Carlitis. After years of under-investment, millions of pounds have been spent on the permanent way. New welded track is in place. (In the

beginning, Barrow Haematite Iron Company contracted to deliver rails to Carnforth at £9.5s a ton). Some of the major viaducts – Ribblehead, Denthead, Smardale - have had major surgery, including the waterproofing the decks. At Settle, the decommissioned signal box was moved away from the tracks and refurbished by cheerful volunteers, who are now on hand at prescribed times to tell visitors about semaphore signalling – a hands-on experience that includes operating the arm of what used to be a distant signal at Blea Moor.

Traffic on the Settle-Carlisle is frequent and varied. Passenger trains maintain a daily service, linking Leeds with Carlisle. A shiver of excitement passes along the lineside and down the spines of train-spotters and photographers when a steam special is advertised. Diverted traffic (from the Lancaster-Carlisle) includes modernistic Virgin trains. The line is much-used by freight traffic, with a goodly number of trains under the auspices of EWS. Gypsum, a by-product of Drax, the largest coal-powered station in Western Europe, is transported by rail to Kirkby Thore near Appleby. Coal imported from various parts of the world is collected by goods train at a Clydeside quay and transported south via the Settle-Carlisle.

The stations that remain look especially well in summer, being festooned with flowers. The waiting room at Settle station is almost a social centre and Christmas here is truly festive, with free drinks, mince pies and cake served in the main waiting room to the accompaniment of live music. Settle and Kirkby Stephen have refurbished footbridges, a safety factor for passengers and a boon to railway photographers seeking a high vantage point when "something special" is expected. The station buildings at Horton-in-Ribblesdale have been restored and adapted for modern use.

Ribblehead has become, under the auspices of Settle-Carlisle Railway Trust, an interpretation centre, with a caretaker's flat. In the grounds is a compact hi-tech weather station that offers an impressive range of information to internet users. A subsidiary of the Railway Trust holds Kirkby Stephen station buildings on a 125-year lease at a peppercorn rent. In 2004, a £350,000 investment in the station buildings at Kirkby Stephen led to the letting of new office suites. At

Langwathby, in the Eden Valley, a café restaurant known as Brief Encounter occupies the main building.

The Friends of the Settle-Carlisle Line, formed at a public meeting in Settle on 27th June, 1981, has a membership of over 3,000 and a host of cheerful volunteers, some of whom act as guides on passenger trains. Other members staff shops at Settle and Appleby. Affixed to an outer wall at Appleby is a plaque commemorating Eric Treacy, former bishop of Wakefield. This outstanding railway photographer collapsed and died at the station, while preparing to photograph a "steam special" on 13th May, 1978. Two years earlier, The Railway Bishop had attended a centenary function in a marquee set up in the yard of Settle station.

The station at Settle with a local stopping train leaving for its trip north. The employee with the barrow seems to have some large packages which have been unloaded from the train. The trackwork still has a cross-over between 'up' and 'down' lines at this time. Passengers head towards the foot crossing as Settle had no footbridge.

Genesis

The Midland Railway, builders of the Settle-Carlisle line, evolved from the Midland Counties Railway Company, based on Derby. The Midland system spread rapidly. From about 1860 the main ambition was to capture the lucrative Scottish passenger and freight traffic, the value of which was well worth the effort. The idea of building a route up the middle of the country, with two north-south valleys and a slab of high Pennine landscape in between, sprang from rivalry with the London and North-Western Railway for a share in that Scottish traffic.

During the 1860s, the Midland – this powerful company intent on expansion – infiltrated on its northward progress the Leeds and Bradford Railway, which had tracks up to Skipton. Trains could be operated as far as Ingleton on the "Little" North-Western Railway but the Ingleton-Lowgill line, a branch of the Lancaster-Carlisle, was controlled by the London and North-Western Railway. To gain access to Scotland for its goods and passengers, the Midland had to hand them over to its rival at Ingleton. Here, Midland passengers were often forced to walk across the gorge of the Greta between the two rival stations, though there was a rail link across the viaduct in between.

James Allport, the Midland's general manager, said it was a very rare thing for him to go down to Carlisle without being turned out twice. He had seen 12 or 15 passengers turned out at Ingleton and the same number at Tebay. "Then, although some of the largest towns in England are on the Midland system, there is no through carriage to Edinburgh, unless we have a family down, and then we make a special arrangement and apply for a special carriage to go through." The Midland had applied in vain for through carriages to Scotland. Mr Allport frequently had letters from passengers complaining that they could not get booked through. "I have sent letters to Mr. Johnson from passengers requiring to come to Derby when booking at Glasgow and they have been told to go by way of Crewe instead of going by Ingleton."

Highest point on the line at Ais Gill and very prone to all weathers. The railway was closed during heavy snow in 1947.

Above: **Hawes Junction for Garsdale. An early view of the station looking north. The period photograph has good examples of station infrastructure, including lighting. An array of elderly Midland carriages wait to progress northwards. The carriages to the right are for a service along the branch to Hawes and beyond to Northallerton.**

Right: Another view of Hawes Junction station taken some years later. Note the signalbox on the 'down' platform. It survives at the same spot today. Passenger trains to Hawes ceased operating in 1953.

Above: **The station at Crosby Garrett. A classic photograph in Edwardian times. Note the road overbridge which spans the whole station and the large station buildings. The stationmaster's house is on the far left.**

Left: **One of Yorkshire's three peaks, Pen-y-gent, features in the background of this view at Helwith Bridge, a few miles north of Settle.**

Opposite page: **The northern portal of Blea Moor tunnel. The tunnel presented one of the most difficult and dangerous structures for the navvies in the mid 1870s. Some 300 miners, bricklayers and labourers worked in the tunnel during the period of construction.**

Left: **A view northwards at Settle Junction. A 'Crosti' boilered Standard Class 9F runs south with a mineral freight train. The train is on the Settle-Carlisle route. The line to the left heads towards Giggleswick and the northern version of Clapham Junction.**

Below: **A goods train takes the 'North Western line' at Settle Junction which connected Leeds with Lancaster. The Settle-Carlisle line was built some 26 years after the line to the right was fully opened. Note the station building on the left. Settle Junction station was built in 1876 and closed a year later!**

In 1865, when hundreds of square miles of the Pennines were without a railway, Lord Wharncliffe, whose properties included a large estate in upper Wensleydale, and several other local gentlemen, proposed a North of England Union Railway. They introduced a Bill to Parliament dealing with the construction of a railway line twixt Settle and Hawes, with a branch from Horton to Clapham, which was on the "Little" North-Western railway. Hawes would be the junction of a branch to Sedbergh and the main line would continue down the dale to join up with systems to the east. The Commons approved the Bill but before the Lords could consider it, the Midland intervened. It was agreed that the Bill should be withdrawn and re-introduced by the Midland in a modified form.

The Midland, actively supported over the Border by two Scottish companies – the North British and the Glasgow and South Western – would lay the tracks from Settle to Hawes. They would continue the major line northwards to Carlisle, which was the gateway to Scotland. When the scheme for a Settle-Carlisle railway was made public in November, great excitement

was generated in the towns and villages of the district. The new Bill, read before the Commons and committed early in 1866 was subsequently approved. As the news reached Appleby, the church bells were rung. The Lords raised no objection and Royal Assent was given on July 16th.

Right: **A very early view of staff at Clapham station on the North Western route to Lancaster. The station opened in 1849 on the route between Skipton and Ingleton. A year later, the line was extended through Bentham and across to Lancaster. In 1861 the branch to Ingleton, which made Clapham a junction station, was extended to Low Gill via Sedbergh.**

Below: **One of two skew bridges crossing the river Ribble at Sherrifs Brow, just north of Stainforth.**
Bob Swallow

Somewhat alarmed, the London and North-Western re-opened talks with the Midland. The outcome was a plan for a joint committee to oversee the working of the Lancaster-Carlisle line. The Midland rejoiced for its finances were being strained by extensions to its system elsewhere. What would be the mood of shareholders if they were asked to approve the raising of a further £2,200,000. The Settle-Carlisle would be an almost unendurable strain on the company's finances. Much rancour had been generated by the Midland decision to "go it alone" on the 72-mile-long middle route to Scotland.

In September, 1866, John Crossley supervised the staking-out of sections of the route – work that was done half-heartedly against talk of abandonment and came to a halt on the last day of the year. The project lay idle for almost two years. When, in 1869, Parliament turned down the Midland's application for an Abandonment Bill, the company shrugged its shoulders and put the work in hand. The Settle-Carlisle was by now enthusiastically supported by landowners who had previously opposed it and also by the Scottish

railway companies. The Midland shareholders voted £550,000 and tenders were invited for four contracts (to cover the construction of a railway between Settle and Carlisle), with a fifth contract for the branch line to Hawes.

The Terrain

The Parliament Act granted the Midland a strip of land. It was left to the company's valuers, through negotiation with the landowners, to acquire it. James Farrer, of Ingleborough Estate, whose land extended over the hill to embrace Blea Moor and Gearstones, had opposed the Settle-Carlisle Bill in 1866. Now he benefited hugely through the sale of land at Batty Moss for the big viaduct that would become known as Ribblehead. Farrer would also draw royalties for quarried stone, for sand and as rent for the land needed for building hutments, temporary quarters for a large labour force, with some wives and children. (As a magistrate, Farrer would become familiar with the wild nature of navvies inflamed by drink).

The impressive viaduct at Crosby Garrett 38 miles south of Carlisle. The structure, and the line, was right on the western edge of the village.

The viaduct structure at Batty Moss (Ribblehead) in the early stages of construction. Most of the stone piers are well advanced and the arches are beginning to be formed. The distinguished Ingleborough peak is visible in the distance on the left.

James Allport and John Crossley made a personal inspection of the route. Crossley then appointed Charles Stanley Sharland, a young Tasmanian engineer, who had a recent association with the Maryport & Carlisle Railway, to make a preliminary survey. Sharland and his helpers completed it in 10 days, despite severe wintry weather. They were snowed up for a time at Gearstones, near Ribblehead. Sharland is said to have tunnelled through a drift to reach a trough containing water. His feats belie poor health yet he developed tuberculosis, retired to balmy Torquay and died in 1871, aged 26 years.

The first sod of the line was cut in November, 1869. Within a week or two a van, grandly known as the Contractors' Hotel, appeared beside Batty Moss, on Contract No 1. Ten men lived in it during the first winter. One of them recalled standing at the door on dark evenings. He held up a bull's eye lantern to guide his fellow workers back to their quarters. The ceremony of cutting "first sods" by local big-wigs appears to have been customary on other contracts. It took place in Mallerstang, on Contract No. 2

There exists a photograph of the Northern Pennines taken from a satellite on which the course of the Settle-Carlisle is clearly shown. From a height of 570 miles, the camera's eye registers several of the main features. Yet at ground level, despite its massive works, the Settle-Carlisle does not dominate its setting. Anyone who follows the old Coal Road between the stations of Garsdale and Dent, which are temporarily out of sight, reaches an elevation of 1,761ft at Shaking Moss. The cackling of red grouse or the melancholic whistle of golden plover breaks the solitude.

At 1,100ft above sea level, Dent is the highest station in England. Badly weathered snow fences, composed of upreared sleepers, accentuate the sense of remoteness. At the approach to Dent, the railway runs on a ledge cut from the lower slopes of Great Knoutberry Hill (2,200ft). During the Second World War, a Spitfire aircraft flew alongside a goods train for a short distance and pilot and guard exchanged greetings by hand-signs.

The same view as the previous picture, but 130 years later. A steam special crosses the 24-arched viaduct in the early 21st century. Little has changed to the landscape in this remote corner of Yorkshire.

The Midland's fast, through, all-weather route to Scotland was a triumph over the many quirks of local topography. A writer in the Carlisle Patriot referred to the central part of the route as "a continued succession of high hills with intervening valleys, so that the line is alternately carried over viaducts or through cuttings or under hills hundreds of feet in height." North Ribblesdale being relatively narrow and steep-sided, there was just one point where the Ribble was crossed, this being just north of Stainforth, where the river's course was adjusted.

On the middle section, where lean fells raked the sky, if the engineers encountered a hill, they drove a tunnel through it. When a bluff was reached, a cutting was made. There would be no variations from the selected route. Every awkward valley was exalted by having a viaduct slung across it. Several million cubic yards of material were poured into quaking bogs. The Eden Valley being vast, fanning out into a plain when close to the Solway, the railway was an insignificant feature, being lost in a vastness between the Lakeland fells and the North Pennines.

The main engineering features were 20 large viaducts and 14 tunnels. In the construction period, the grim weather slowed up progress. Embankments cracked and slipped. Glaciers of the Pleistocene Age that had conveniently gouged the tiny valleys into major dales, providing the only conceivable route for the Settle-Carlisle, smeared the sides with boulder clay which, when disturbed, was hard as concrete in dry weather. In wet conditions it had the consistency of Yorkshire pudding mixture.

No one doubted that the most difficult stretch would lie between Blea Moor and Aisgill, a distance of 10 miles through what the old-time topographer Camden had called a "horrid silent wilderness". In this wilderness, for example, the boundary of Mallerstang parish ran "thence to a hurrock of stones at the east end of Swarth Fell, called Swarth Fell Pike, thence to a hurrock of stones in Galloway Gates, thence as Heaven water deals to Blandston…"

Junction, where the line began, is situated nearer to Long Preston than was first intended. The railway ran on hillsides rather than dale bottoms, being laid on ledges cut from lonely fells and across high-arched bridges at the gills.

The Eden Valley, with its outcrops of new red sandstone, has a warm appearance, contrasting with the dazzling but hard limestone terrain of North Ribblesdale. The scenery beside the Eden Gorge – with its heather and pinewoods – has affinities with the Scottish Highlands. Three tunnels and three viaducts adorn this tract of land at the approach to Carlisle. Making them was not especially difficult – until a landslip occurred where the railway was set on a customary hillside

Construction well underway at Crowdundle. The wooden formers were fabricated to allow the arch to be constructed out of local stone. Men are seen working on the king pier and a crane is present.

Crossing the watershed was a dominant thought in the minds of engineers. With a ruling gradient of 1 in 100, the railway must begin to climb immediately at Settle Junction (in the south) and also in the Appleby area (to the north) if the 1,169ft of Aisgill Moor was to be cleared comfortably. Settle

ledge at Edenbrows, between Armathwaite and High Stand Gill. Five acres of ground were affected. Binding what remained gave the engineers many problems. After crossing the river at Eden Lacy viaduct, the line runs on the western side for the rest of the way to Carlisle.

When the work was done, a newspaper observed: "Perhaps nowhere in the kingdom has nature placed such gigantic obstacles in the way of the railway engineers as have been encountered over the 72 miles lying between Settle and Carlisle." The Pennine climate, characterised by a cold late spring, cloudy and moist summer, a settled autumn and a hard, long winter, was to test the resolution of those who made the Settle-Carlisle railway once the navvy force had departed. The Helm Wind is a fearful draught brewed up about High Cup Nick, on the northern Pennines. It was known to blow coal from the shovel of a fireman in the act of performing his work.

A writer in The Westmorland Gazette became lyrical as he announced the railway was open to passengers: "Much of the scenery traversed is exceedingly beautiful and the change from the wild moorland and fells of the southern part of the line to the highly-cultivated and Devonshire-like Eden Valley is extremely striking. Parts of the Eden Valley are singularly picturesque. A point called Edenbrow, where there has been great difficulty with a land-slip, almost reproduces the Garry and Killiecrankie. For seeing these beauties, the Pullman cars and the new rolling stock offer great advantages, their windows allowing a wider range of outlook than can be obtained from a common carriage."

The little church in Chapel-le-Dale, just a few miles west of Batty Moss. This remote church is host to numerous graves of navvies who fell in service during the building of the railway.

Midland Men

James Joseph Allport, who had been the Midland's general manager since 1853, had a comfortable start in life and a prestigious end - a knighthood. This son of a Birmingham small arms manufacturer, educated in Belgium, had been lured by the Midland from another railway company with the offer of a salary of £1,500 a year. A bold man, who became known as the "Bismark of Railway Politics", he shuddered when, visiting the high hills where the Settle-Carlisle was to go, he became aware of the difficulties surrounding the undertaking.

He recalled his feelings when, at the completion of the line, he was presented with a portrait, requesting that the background should feature Blea Moor. He and Crossley, the engineer, walked over the greater part of the route the line would take. They found it "comparatively easy sailing until we got to that terrible place, Blea Moor." Allport, tireless worker and great innovator, retired in 1880 with a handsome cheque from the Midland shareholders. He received his knighthood four years later.

The man with the unenviable task of reporting to the shareholders on the progress of the line was Edward Shipley Ellis, deputy chairman of the Midland from May, 1870, and chairman from May 1873 until his death in December, 1879. He toured the course of the line to inspect progress for himself. John Sydney Crossley, as the Midland's engineer, was ordered to prepare the plans for the Settle-Carlisle when the Midland Board met on August 2, 1865. In autumn of the following year he was staking out portions of the proposed line. This astonishing man, who by his skills and drive made the Settle-Carlisle his own, and who even designed the graceful viaducts, was born at Loughborough on Christmas Day, 1812, being orphaned two years later. His feverish railway activity led to him having a paralytic stroke, which he overcame largely by force of personality.

One of the Midland's greatest viaducts on the Settle-Carlisle was here at Arten Gill. Peter Fox

Just before Crossley could concentrate on the Settle-Carlisle, storms destroyed a viaduct at Apperley Bridge. Its replacement was expected to take six months, but Crossley had traffic running again in five weeks. He prepared the estimates on which contracts for the Settle-Carlisle were based. His monthly reports on progress in appalling weather conditions, and with a fickle labour force, in turn chilled and cheered the Midland directors. Crossley delayed his retirement from the Midland to see the line through to completion.

Ill-health caused him to resign shortly before completion but he was retained as a consultant. His wife Agnes laid the last stone in the Smardale Viaduct in June 1875. Crossley died on 10 June, 1879. The Hawes branch had been opened. The grand scheme that was largely a tribute to Crossley was complete.

Engineers

Part of the appeal of the Settle-Carlisle would lie in the devil-may-care attitude adopted by the engineers. They faced rough and mountainous terrain without blanching. O S Nock, a celebrated writer on railway topics, noted that "this line is the only mountain railway in the world that was built for express trains." In the autumn of 1869, engineers and their men arrived at the head of Ribblesdale, which would be the setting for some of the largest works. Their office and sleeping accommodation was a horse-drawn caravan which reputedly had travelled from London.

Construction began early in the following year. As noted, one engineer compared the profile of the Settle-Carlisle with a whale "lying on its belly, with its nose in Settle and its tail in Carlisle." This whale measures 22 miles from nose to crown of head and a further 50 miles from here to the tip of its tail. A ruling gradient of 1 in 100 having been fixed, and the watershed at Aisgill being 1,169ft, the engineers were concerned about it from the very beginning at Settle Junction. They must gain an elevation of no less than 740 ft.

Use was made of handy material. A particularly hard rock taken from Anley Cutting was ideal for making bridges in the locality. Birkbeck, a banker, who lived at Anley, is said to have been so concerned when the Midland engineers proposed to demolish his favourite little bridge that he sat on it, day and night. Their ruse to make him leave the bridge was to send a man to him with news of a "run" on the Craven Bank at Settle. Birkbeck went to investigate. While he was away the bridge was demolished. At Sheriff Brow, near Stainforth, where two viaducts were planned, permission was gained from the landowner to divert the river.

They grappled with boulder clay, a legacy of the glacial period during which the valleys were deepened. A despairing engineer told the Midland historian, F S Williams: "I have

Early 20th century railwaymen keeping the track formation up to standard.

known the men blast the boulder clay like rock and within a few hours have to ladle out the same stuff from the same spot like soup in buckets. Or a man strikes a blow with his pick at what he thinks is clay but there is a great boulder underneath almost as hard as iron. The man's wrists, arms and body are so shaken by the shock that, disgusted, he flings down his tools, asks for his money – and is off."

The viaduct at the dalehead was originally called Batty Green, after the locality, but now has the title of Ribblehead viaduct. It was to be built from north to south, using a dark limestone that outcropped in Littledale for the piers and facing stones. The underside of the arches would be completed using locally produced bricks. Discussions took place about the extent of the flanking embankments in relation to the viaduct. The crucial factor was available labour. At first, 18 arches were proposed. Then, with the level of manpower on hand, the scheme was modified to 24 arches, with each sixth pier made a "king" so that, in the event of unforeseen damage, only five piers would be liable to collapse.

The engineers maintained the 1 in 100 gradient across the viaduct to within the south portals of the 2,629 yard Blea Moor Tunnel. Aware of the stresses on those who would nurse steam locomotives up the Drag and into a damp tunnel where locomotive wheels might slip, a kinder gradient of 1 in 440 was adopted. The miners who excavated this tunnel worked at a depth of up to 500ft when passing under "the Crag of Blea Moor". Opening up the ends and headings from seven shafts, miners had primitive tools and a new type of explosive known as dynamite. Work went on by night and day – though not on Sunday – by candlelight. Steam-driven winding engines and large buckets were used to lower men into the "bowels" of the hill and to remove the spoil from the workings.

From the north portal of Blea Moor tunnel, for the next six miles, the Settle-Carlisle runs on the 1,100 ft contour. Engineers and masons grappled with the problems of spanning deep gills with bridges and viaducts, the notable viaducts being Dent Head and Arten Gill. Rise Hill, a mile beyond Dent station, was tunneled for almost a mile in the same forthright way as Blea Moor. It is not quite straight, curving a little at the northern end. An embankment was

Remembering the engineers on the Settle-Carlisle: A plaque beneath the viaduct at Ribblehead. Several hundred navvies lost their lives building the railway to Carlisle.
Peter Fox

proposed for the mossland at the head of Garsdale but after tipping material for two years, Dandry Mire viaduct came into being.

Beyond Aisgill Moor the line was not to swerve at Birkett Common. A cutting driven through shale, and a tunnel 424 yards long, maintained the hillside situation. Consequently, Kirkby Stephen station appeared on a hill over two miles from the centre of the town. On the long descent into the Eden Valley, the ruling gradient was sustained. Appleby, county town of Westmorland, had its importance further enhanced by a station that would be a stopping place for some of the crack expresses. In the Eden Valley, the line plays hide-and-seek with the northward-flowing river. The engineers also had to contend with peeved estate owners, including Mr Crackenthorpe of Newbiggin Hall. The Midland historian, F S Williams, recorded that when it was proposed to drive the railway through a tract of old woodland on the Newbiggin estate, its owner requested that the finest of the oak trees should be spared. He might use it to "hang you and all the Engineers of the Midland Railway upon it, for daring to come here at all."

Contractors

A Victorian contractor needed steady nerves from the moment he proffered a tender. In the run-up to the beginning of work, estimates and prices were set down and altered to suit changing circumstances. The documents for Contract No 1 – Settle Junction to Dent Head, a distance of 17 miles, 18 chains - signed by John Ashwell in November 1869 give an insight into what was expected. He would provide all the material (except the stations and permanent way) needed for a double line. He was to pay his men at least once a fortnight. He would be responsible for maintaining a police presence as required by the local magistrates. The only Sunday working to be allowed would be claimed on completion. As far as he was concerned, this never happened. In October, 1871, Ashwell was in a financial plight. The Midland took over the work with W H Ashwell, one of his agents, in charge.

On Contract No 1, workshops were built on Batty Green. Hutments were set down for the work force and dependants, by no means all of whom could get lodgings locally. A tramway was constructed to take material to Blea Moor and to transport dressed stone from Littledale. Along it also would be taken coal for the steam engines at the head of the nearest shafts. Batty Green, which had been a desolate stretch of

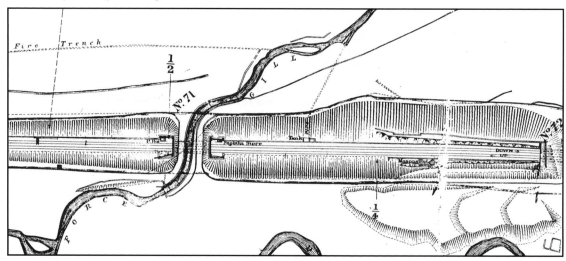

be that specifically requested by the company's engineer. Dates were set for the completion of specified work; an over-run would lead to a penalty of £20 a day.

Ashwell, of Highgate Road, Kentish Town, who secured his contract for £348,318, was soon having sleepless nights as he pondered over problems relating to recruitment of workers and incessant foul weather. On his stretch were Ribblehead Viaduct and Blea Moor Tunnel. His agents were James Hope and William H Ashwell. The Midland wisely split this contract into two with regard to supervision, appointing R E Wilson and E O Ferguson to the southern and northern sections respectively. Ashwell agreed to take half the money as the shafts for Blea Moor Tunnel were being sunk. The remainder

boggy land, was soon bustling with life. The social needs of the navvy families were recognised with the building of a mission house and there was also a wood-framed hospital which was extended during a smallpox outbreak. The second Mr Ashwell, concerned about the welfare of the labour force, had shelters erected for masons working on the viaduct. He retained the typical Victorian consciousness of class. Presiding over a Penny Reading at Batty Green in 1873, he said: "There is honour due to the Batty Wife Greeners, inasmuch as they are able to furnish such talent from the lower and working classes."

Contract No 2, from Dent Head to Smardale, a distance of 17 miles, went to Messrs Benton and Woodiwiss at £334,880.

The resident engineer was John S Storey. Contract No 3, Smardale to Newbiggin, 15 miles, was awarded to Joseph Firbank at £278,813. His agent was J Throstle and the resident engineer Jessie Drage. Contract No 4, from Newbiggin to Carlisle, a distance of 24 miles, was awarded to Messrs Eckersley & Bayliss at £329,905, the contractor's agents being J Lambert and E Williams. The resident engineers were John Allin, Samuel S Paine and Dr Head. Contact No 5 went to Messrs Benton and Woodiwiss at £83,913 12s 6d. The resident engineers were Frank Lynde and Edward Newcombe.

Among the sub-contractors was Job Hirst, who was involved with masonry, from the imposing viaduct to lesser bridges and the near portals of Blea Moor. A Yorkshireman, born in 1815 at Kirkheaton near Huddersfield, he was taught the business of building "long bridges" when he was employed as a stone mason. His competence led him to Wales, thence to India, where he constructed the viaducts and excavated the tunnels for the Bombay to Poona Railway, the first to be built in India. At Ribblehead, Job Hirst employed 52 men, a workforce that soon rose to 150 at the viaduct and 28 men at an aqueduct on Blea Moor.

Job cared for his workforce. Socially inclined, he took part in the "penny readings", variety events that were popular in winter. In summer, Job helped to organise sports days. He did not live to see the completion of the Settle-Carlisle. In December, 1872, aged 57, he was mugged when returning with horse and trap from Ingleton, where he had collected wages for his men. His daughter, Nancy Ellen Hirst gave an account of his death to her niece, Gwenllian Hirst, who recorded what happened in 1963: "Grandfather had gone to Ingleton in a horse and trap from Ribblehead, where the family lived in a house built for them by the Midland Railway by the source of the Ribble…In a snowstorm, on the return journey, he was set upon by thieves, who took the wages and grandfather's gold watch, leaving him unconscious by the side of the road."

When Job regained consciousness, the horse was stationary with the trap nearby. Seeing something glittering by a stile close at hand, he found his watch hanging by its chain in the bushes. Job had no sooner climbed into the trap than he again lost consciousness. His wife, who had stayed up late in anticipation of his return, heard the horse's steps and, going outdoors, found him on the floor of the trap. The horse had brought him home. When he revived, she gave him a glass of port but in the morning she found him dead in bed beside her. "The doctor said he died of an apoplectic fit and the port was the worst thing he could have had."

Job was interred in the yard of Chapel-le-Dale church, where a memorial of ornate, inscribed stone with a cross was raised above his grave. On the day of his funeral, all the shops at Batty Green were closed and the blinds of every window in the shanties were drawn down. The labour force peaked at about 6,000. It was a fickle force, with many comings and goings. The number was at its lowest in the deep midwinter. It also dipped in summer when some of the men returned to their home farms to help with the haymaking. John deLacy Duffy, civil engineer and manager for Mr Ashwell on Contract No 1, was especially concerned with bridges at the southern end of the line. Duffy employed many Irishmen and was annoyed when English workers threatened them. In 1871, when he cautioned a miner that beer was not to be sold in the huts without a licence, the angry man threatened to murder him.

Permanent way staff in the early 20th century somewhere between Settle and Ribblehead.
Veronica Parker collection

Labourers

The construction of the Settle-Carlisle is popularly thought of as a navvy operation. The navvy was a lowly if common member of a skilful, varied team, with a score of categories. For instance, before masons could work on a viaduct, joiners had to provide wooden scaffolding. Not even a workforce numbering thousands could have completed the project in six years without some machines. The mason on his viaduct used hammer and trowel but the heavy stone blocks, some weighing over five tons, were delivered to him on the decking by a steam-operated "traveller". In former days, six men might labour for an hour to lift a single stone into place. Masons on the Settle-Carlisle saw the "traveller" do equivalent work in a few minutes, smoothly lifting a stone for 70ft or more.

Fixed steam engines, assembled at the head of tunnel shafts on Blea Moor or Rise Hill, hauled up to the surface material excavated from the headings. Steam locomotives with rakes of trucks chugged on tramways laid across wild areas. The navvy might still need his shovel but other workers supervised tip-wagons containing material excavated from cuttings. The stuff was disposed precisely where it was needed on a budding embankment.

Many horses were available to haul carts laden with spoil from the tunnels or taking provisions and equipment across rough ground. Ordinary carts could not be used on the boggy Batty Green so a variation of a cart as used on soggy agricultural land came into use. This "bog cart" consisted of a huge barrel supporting a cart frame. The poor horses sometimes foundered or lost their shoes in the wet ground. In summer, fresh grazing for the horses was plentiful. In winter, the animals were given hay, beans and oats. Even here, an element of mechanisation was to be seen. An ingenious engine set up at Kirkby Stephen cut or crushed the horses' food – and could then be adapted for sawing wood! Dynamite, a novelty when used on the Settle-Carlisle, shattered the hardest rock.

In the early 1870s, the weather more than lived up to its reputation. Masons feared the high winds to which they were

Cottages developed by the Midland Railway for its workers. This is the set of sturdy houses at Moorcock, just to the north of Garsdale station. Nothing as sophisticated was given to the navvies during the construction period who had to cope with temporary shanty accommodation.

exposed as they bestrode the wooden frames surrounding the emergent piers on viaducts. Work was hampered by torrential rain, when torrents rushed into the ends of partly completed tunnels. At Dent Head during 1872 there were 92 inches of rain compared with the average of 68 inches. At Kirkby Stephen, 60 inches of rain were recorded against an average of 37.

In the deep mid-winter, the fell country was snowbound and frosted for months on end. A minor earthquake shook the huts standing on the wild face of Blea Moor. In 1874, a man who toured the still incomplete works commented on unfavourable remarks by some at the slow rate of progress. He wrote: "Let them go over it in the drenching rain of October…wade through mire, clay and water, and see the slurry spreading far beyond the company's boundaries." A writer in Wildman's Household Almanack in 1874 noted: "The 'slurry' slips out of the embankments and sticks to the tip wagons, often causing these to come badly over the 'tip head' and damaging it greatly; besides the expense of getting the wagon again on the embankment some 60 feet up." The clay on Batty Moss was found to be free from limestone pebbles and so it was used for making the bricks needed for lining the arches of Ribblehead viaduct and for reinforcing sections of Blea Moor tunnel.

The workers demonstrated that not only faith moves mountains. They created some impressive embankments. About 250,000 cubic yards of ballast formed the high embankment just north of Settle. Some 100,000 cubic yards of "slurry" were removed to make a cutting near Horton-in-Ribblesdale. Intake Embankment, above Mallerstang, 400 yards long and 75 feet high at the centre, absorbed 260,000 cubic yards of material.

David Page, medical officer of Health in the Sedbergh Rural Sanitary District, was concerned at the condition of the hutment at Dent Head. He found navvies, miners, their families and lodgers were occupying the wooden huts. The structures had been set on a patch of bogland that had been made "almost untraversable by reason of the state of puddle it is in from surface water and refuse matter thrown out immediately from the doorways. Planks laid over this

The first stages in the construction of Ribblehead viaduct. The piers are starting to rise from Batty Green and you can see the shanty town for navvies and their families in the background.

quagmire and stepping-stones afford access to some of the huts. There is no vestige of drainage save the open trenches cut round the walls of the huts to protect them from inundation."

The dour weather and the tedium of life in remote areas led to alcoholism in the hutments. The excise officers had not sanctioned most of the liquor consumed. Snooping on railway huts was an unsavoury part of a policeman's task. An official who was a stranger in the district could obtain evidence of drink being supplied without a licence. He might order drink and then charge the individual who supplied it. The local bobby and a colleague who watched through the window of a hut at Crow Hill, near Helm, saw a pint of ale being supplied to Charles Walker, who threw down half-a-crown in payment. The landlady gave him two shillings in change. When the constable entered the hut, Walker was quaffing his ale and James Whitehead, a drunken landlord, was sitting in the kitchen. The Appleby Bench fined Whitehead for selling beer without a licence. In May, 1873, the inn at Gearstones was badly damaged when a navvy playfully threw a charge of dynamite on the kitchen fire.

Viaducts

The majestic viaduct at Ribblehead viewed in the 1990s. Whernside is the peak in the background.   Roger Hardingham

The viaducts of the Settle-Carlisle, built to John Crossley's graceful design, have a strong visual appeal. None is more prominent than Ribblehead, the piers of which are set deeply in Batty Moss. Immense embankments buttress the 24 arches. The viaduct has a length of 1,328 yards. So great was the planned structure that work on it began immediately the contract was signed. Trial borings took place during the winter of 1869-70. Shafts were sunk through peat and clay to the solid rock. A story began to circulate that the piers were being support by bales of wool.

The viaduct was built from north to south, using mainly Welsh masons. About 100 men worked on the structure at any given time and in March 1872 they were on strike for a week for better wages. The outcome is not known but previously they had been paid 6s. 3d for a nine-hour day and 6s 11d for 10 hours in summer. Much thought went into the selection of the stone. In due course, a stream in Littledale was diverted to expose the finest beds of rock, which yielded over 30,000 cubic yards of material. Stone was borne to its destination by tramway. An engine was used for mixing the mortar. Sand needed for two viaducts and the tunnel came from a quarry on the heights of Blea Moor.

The piers that emerged from the shafts were enmeshed in a light timber stage to facilitate building and also to enable the builders to use a "steam traveller", to lift the blocks of limestone to their appointed places. The timbering was done in sections. When the arches of one group had been turned, the timbers were moved to where more piers were emerging from the moor. The 45ft spans were assembled on wooden framing and when each frame was removed the arch (it was claimed) dropped a mere quarter of an inch. The arches were then covered with concrete and, in turn, overlaid with asphalt to deflect water from the brick lining. Bricks were made locally both for the viaduct and for Blea Moor tunnel. Such bricks were unsatisfactory. Those exposed to weathering were replaced in due course by Accrington reds and other hard varieties of brick.

Dent Head, north of Blea Moor, has 10 spans, a length of 596ft and a maximum height of 100 feet. A "blue" variety of limestone, quarried locally, was used for the work. Arten Gill viaduct, spanning the next gill northwards, has piers that look impossibly slender, each pier being 15ft thick at the bottom and much narrower at the top. When the builders were questing for bedrock they had to sink shafts to a depth of over 50ft for some of the piers. A dark, highly fossilised limestone known as Dent Marble went into its construction. Because sand was unobtainable locally, the mortar was made of lime and burnt clay, being referred to as "Crossley Cement". The arches were turned using stone, not brick. The v-shaped gill was bedecked by a 660ft long viaduct having 11 spans and soaring to a maximum height of 117ft.

One viaduct was built in desperation. Dandry Mire makes a 12-span crossing of what used to be a notorious moss. The original plan was to create an embankment but Dandry Mire had an insatiable appetite for tipped material. Every tip wagon taken to the area had to be conveyed by road to Sedbergh and the carriage on each was a guinea. A hundred wagons were in regular use and tipping went on for two years. The continuous wet weather and the sogginess of the mire merely caused the peat to rise up on either side. Banks that were 12 feet wide appeared. One bank extended 24 yards beyond the Midland's boundary. In 1872, frustrated engineers decided to build a viaduct. At the time this

Above: **Construction of Dent Head viaduct is underway using local stone from two large quarries on the nearby hillside.**
Below: **Smardale viaduct has 12 arches and is 130 feet above the level of the river. The 'last' stone was put in place by Agnes Crossley during a ceremony on 8th June 1875.**

A scene from above the tunnel at Blea Moor showing one of the vents constructed to allow navvies access to the tunnel workface and ultimately used to allow smoke from engines escape from within the one and a half-mile long tunnel. The railway line can be seen as it leaves the northern end of the tunnel and crosses over Dent Head viaduct. Roger Hardingham

decision was taken the nearby Moorcock viaduct was complete apart from the coping stones.

The 12-arch Smardale viaduct, in the Eden Valley, was the tallest, at 130ft above the level of Scandal Beck. Some of the trial boreholes probed for 20 feet to the underlying rock. The viaduct absorbed 60,000 tons of limestone. The original design included a second set of six arches at a lower level and between two hefty piers. The engineers confidently dispensed with the idea. There were early difficulties at 10-arch Ormside viaduct, where the railway crosses the Eden for the first time. One of the piers had to stand in the river, so the engineers made a miniature coffer dam of inch board. To find a satisfactory foundation for a pier on the north side of the river, the ground had to be excavated to a depth of 34ft. A coffer dam, at Eden Lacy, near Little Salkeld, was destroyed when the river went into spate in 1872. Crowdundle was built of freestone across a beck that, in "railway time", was part of the boundary between Cumberland and Westmorland.

Tunnels

View Blea Moor from afar and you see the old tramways winding between heaps of rock blasted at the heart of the hill and raised up the shafts by steam-winch during over four years of tunnelling. Blea Moor tunnel, which is 2,629 yards long, is the most famous on the Settle-Carlisle. The ventilation shafts break the moorland surface as circular structures of brick. They are like red pimples on the hill's rugged pate. Fine mesh prevents foreign bodies from descending to the railway tracks hundreds of feet below. Years ago, when I joined an inspection party, I viewed the shafts from below. These brick-lined tubes, 10ft in diameter, gleamed with moisture. Garlands had been placed at intervals to catch water and lead it into fallpipes from which it would flow into the main drains.

The tunnelling project, which was as severe as any task on the line, cost £45 a yard. Relays of men endured gloomy, wet conditions. Tramway and winches were needed to take material to the hilltop, where the shafts would be driven, the first being the most northerly. The "iron road" laid by the contractor for two and a-half miles from Batty Moss was for light engines and trucks. They were supplanted on steeper ground by a tramway operated by a wire rope that was connected to a fixed engine. Another tramway was self-acting, the weight of trucks bearing millstone grit from a local quarry being more than sufficient to draw up strings of empty trucks.

Seven stationary engines were needed on and around Blea Moor, two of them winding up materials on either side of the hill, as aforementioned, and the others being placed at the heads of the shafts to remove debris from the workings far below, this being done in steps. Men employed at the headings and the bricks and mortar needed for lining sections of the tunnel were lowered and raised. Appliances pumped water from the completed sections and supplied air to the workers. The fuel for all this machinery was coal, conveyed up the Moor first by donkeys and then, with railtrack in situ, in trolleys. The coal was often crowned with bags of flour and other domestic commodities for the workers and their families who lived in huts.

Miners, the folk heroes of Blea Moor, worked by candlelight. At the peak of activity about 300 miners, bricklayers and labourers worked here. The bill for tallow candles averaged £50 a month. Holes for the explosives were drilled by hand. Dynamite, then a novelty, was packed into the holes and ignited by means of a time fuse, the bill for dynamite being £200 a ton. A major part of this cost was

A view looking south through the portal of Blea Moor tunnel. The bridge in the distance in an aqueduct carrying Force Gill.

A view from the aqueduct bridge looking north into the tunnel mouth of Blea Moor. The mounds of spoil on the right were created from the vast quantities of rock removed from the mining of the tunnel in the 1870s. Roger Hardingham

transportation by road from Newcastle to Carlisle. The existing railway companies would not take the risk of handling it. Material displaced at the ends of the tunnel was removed in trolleys hauled by well-groomed horses. Their proud drivers bedecked the steeds with ribbon.

During the excavation of Blea Moor tunnel less than a dozen serious accidents were recorded. Recesses were made to act as refuges for the maintenance men, the deepest of them being known as the "donkey hole". Many years later, when loop lines were installed at Blea Moor and an outer distant signal was placed in the tunnel, a gong was installed as a warning device. It never worked properly and was removed when the signal was re-positioned outside the tunnel.

A man who was in the Blea Moor maintenance gang for 13 years lived during that time at one of the local cottages, not far from the signal box and more than a mile from Ribblehead. The Chapel-le-Dale postman, operating on foot, delivered

letters for Blea Moor. The family shopping was carried out in Settle, groceries being ordered and delivered to Ribblehead station once a month. From here, the groceries were transported to Blea Moor by the stopping freight train. This railwayman, a Methodist local preacher, often carried his bicycle across Ribblehead viaduct at the start of a journey to a local chapel. When he was planned to preach at Dent he would carry it through Blea Moor Tunnel. He knew the times of the trains and "there wasn't much traffic on a Sunday." His wife had more than once crossed the viaduct at Ribblehead with her baby in her arms when walking to Ribblehead to catch a train for Settle.

Blea Moor has stolen much of the glamour from an impressive tunnel bored through Rise Hill, north of Dent station. At 1,213ft it was a baby compared with Blea Moor but it inherited some of its awkward traits, being remote from roads and villages. Two air shafts were excavated. The deepest of them penetrated the hill for 147 yards. Workmen at the Rise Hill workings were hauled up from Garsdale in bogies on a tramway three-quarters of a mile long that was operated by steam engine. The tramway was not for their exclusive use, of course, being also used to carry coal, railway material and provisions.

At Rise Hill, the excavated hillside material, which was little more than slush in places, adhered to the implements like treacle, being removed with the help of grafting tools and buckets of water. Care had to be taken when rock was blasted because pieces weighing 15 cwt were known to fly a distance of 20 yards. A visitor to Rise Hill saw dimly burning candles, uncouth-looking wagons standing on the rails or moving to and fro and men at the facings "with their numerous lights like twinkling stars in a hazy night". It was a noisy place, especially the noise made by twirling drills beneath "the terrible force of big hammers wielded by stalwart men, the hac-hac or half-sepulchral groan at each stroke, the murky vapour, the chilling damp and the thick breathing."

Birkett Tunnel, 424 yards in length, lies on a fault line and in its construction the miners dealt with shale, magnesium limestone, mountain limestone, grit, slate, iron, coal and a workable vein of lead. There was an alarming rock fall. John Crossley, the Midland's chief engineer, on being shown this geological hotch-potch, remarked that he had not seen a more curious combination. When Helm tunnel, 600 yards long, was completed in 1875, the entire space was brilliantly illuminated and engineers and local people assembled, in the Victorian way, for mutual congratulation. Culgaith tunnel, 661 yards, was driven through hard red marl but only one ventilation shaft was needed.

The line emerges into daylight near the river Eden and the two are never more than a mile apart until beyond Cotehill. The railway is in the open air for only a quarter of a mile before it vanishes into Waste Bank tunnel, which is extremely short. A cutting might have sufficed but the engineers, fearing landslip, decided to leave it roofed in. Like all the tunnels north of this point, it was cut through red sandstone. Some culverts were almost large enough to be classified as tunnels. The Keld Beck culvert assists a flow of water into the upper Dee and, the ground being steep, it was stepped. Cow Gill, which is crossed by a 100ft embankment, has a culvert 540ft long; it is shaped like a Gothic arch.

Above: **Roughly half way between Dent Head and the station at Dent is this unusual culvert at Kell Beck. The main span is 10ft 6in. It spanned a small valley.**
Below: **Several tunnels along the route were hewn from extreme geological obstacles. The huge rocks surrounding this tunnel entrance illustrate the task facing the miners in forming these structures.** Bob Swallow

Motive power

Engine driver John Mayblin of Carlisle drove a re-built Kirtley 2-4-0 (No. 806), in dark green livery, when the first passenger train used the Settle-Carlisle in the Spring of 1876. Matthew Kirtley, its designer, had been a dominant figure in the build-up of the Midland system for about a quarter of a century. He devised a way of burning coal rather than coke in a locomotive. He was involved with Allport and Crossley in the planning and operation of motive power on the new railway – 2-4-0 for passenger traffic and 0-6-0 for freight. He agreed with Crossley on the conclusions of a report to the construction committee dealing with sites for engine sheds and stations. And, alas, he died in 1873, before the Settle-Carlisle was operative.

Kirtley locomotives performed well but had spartan cabs, exposing footplate crews to the vagaries of Pennine weather.

Samuel Johnson introduced the graceful Compounds that succeeded Kirtleys. By this time the Midland had its familiar red livery and the 2-4-0s had been relegated to local and pilot work. Under Johnson, Midland loco policy was switched from outside-frame engines to types with inside frames. The original size of locomotive lacked power as the weight of coaching stock increased in weight and size, especially following the introduction of Pullman cars.

When Johnson retired from office in 1903, Richard Deeley became the last of an outstanding trio of Midland locomotive engineers. Deeley improved existing locomotives and designed 10 specifically for the Settle-Carlisle route. With their distinctive beat, the Compounds were the mainstay on the passenger services north of Leeds in the first half of the 20th century. So popular were they that the LMS built another 195

Top of the line - Ais Gill summit in the early part of the 20th century. A Midland 4-4-0 hauls a train southwards.

Right: **The change-over years. From the footplate of a BR Standard class locomotive waiting in the siding, a diesel-hauled freight train heads north through Horton-in-Ribblesdale. The siding led to the limestone quarry.**

Below: **The only surviving Midland compound locomotive, No. 1000, heads a train up towards Ais Gill with LMS Jubilee class No. 5690** Leander. **The compound is part of the National Collection at York's railway museum.**

A scene at Garsdale with a Standard Class 2-6-0 locomotive. The tank house, since demolished, dominates the photograph.

Compounds after Grouping in 1923. (Some were still in use under the auspices of British Railways).

In the twilight of steam, Jubilees and Staniers, not forgetting the giant Pacifics, stormed the Settle-Carlisle. William Stanier, who became the Chief Locomotive Superintendent of the LMS in 1932, was responsible for the highly successful 5XP Jubilee 4-6-0 and the Black Five 4-6-0. After teething troubles, the Jubilees became masters of the line, hauling passenger trains between Leeds and Carlisle for the next 30 years. In 1943, the first of the re-built Scots, which had taper boilers, were put in service on the Settle-Carlisle. For the remainder of the Steam Age these powerful locomotives hauled most of the express trains.

John Mason, who was born four years after the line to Hawes was opened, and was employed at this station from

1900 until his retirement many years later, remembered when pride was everywhere evident. A man might use a certain locomotive for most of his railway career. The footplate men made their engines shine through frequent cleaning. John had known a fireman leave the footplate as soon as Hawes was reached so that he might polish the brass work and clean and oil other sections of the engine.

Some locomotives were personalised. Bonnyface was the nickname for an express that ran between Bradford and Hawes. Limey an evening train, took limestone from the Ribblesdale quarries into Scotland. The final British Railways steam special over the Settle-Carlisle, on August 11th 1968, was hauled by No. 70013 Oliver Cromwell and two ex-LMS Black Fives (44781 and 44871). In the Steam Revival of the 1980s, both the 9F 2-10-0 No. 92220 Evening Star and 4-6-2 No. 4472 Flying Scotsman made a number of return journeys.

A Black Five locomotive heads a local service towards the south over Ribblehead viaduct. These locomotives were commonplace over the route right up until the end of steam in 1968.

For half a century, the ubiquitous 0-6-0 handled freight traffic. Midland and LMS railways produced hundreds of this type. From the late 1930s, freight was being moved by the mixed traffic engine nicknamed "Crab" and by the ever-willing Black Fives. In the early 1960s, and before the end of working Steam, diesel locomotives undertook most of the Settle-Carlisle passenger workings. The Class 45 Peak became the mainstay of the line, three of the locomotives having been named after the Three Peaks – Whernside, Ingleborough and Pen-y-ghent. The longest spell of service was by Class 47s. They were produced in large numbers.

Drivers

A veteran driver on the Settle-Carlisle remarked: "I don't think there's another section of railway in this country where the regulator had to be kept open for so long. You got your Midnight Express from Carlisle to Aisgill in about 1 hour and 3 minutes. It was about 11 minutes across t'top. That's about an hour and a quarter – and you hadn't shut that regulator." A driver who was "only t'size o' two pennorth o' copper" and perched rather than sat on his seat was hard on the regulator. When he was driving, he jerked it. "That regulator was either open or shut. He used to go through some coal." A Hellifield man who never exceeded 30 miles an hour in his car could not go fast enough when driving an engine. The driver of a goods train out of Carlisle turned his cap round to reflect his passion for speed. The signalmen let him go. "We rang all the way up. He came by, waving. The old brake van was waddling about. He got to Hellifield, seventy-six miles, in just over 80 minutes."

The men who thrashed the steam-hauled trains from the south knew the first 22 miles of the "Carlisle road" as The

Goods trains spent much of their time in the sidings, letting the passenger trains go through. One driver would disappear from the footplate for 40 minutes, knowing that the train was unlikely to be cleared in less time. His fireman discovered that he knew the location of every lineside pub.

Firemen

A fireman on the Settle-Carlisle was only as good as the quality of his coal. "It was a mixed grill, was coal. You couldn't expect anything else, I suppose. A lot of it was rubbish. In 1963, I knew locos that left light engine to go to Blea Moor for snow ploughing. They had to clean the fire when they got there. Dirty coal!" Yorkshire pit coal was the best yet Yorkshire "hards", while theoretically coal, looked and acted like slate. "When you hit it with a hammer it broke up in layers. When you put it on t'fire, it just crackled. There's been a few signal boxes on fire due to Yorkshire 'hards'." If you got some Welsh coal, you couldn't get much steam. "It was only good for throwing at rabbits."

Two footplatemen on board an LMS locomotive at Carlisle station in 2008. Frank Santrian, on the right, worked more than 60 years with steam.

Drag. It was short and sharp - "blood for money". The driver of a steam locomotive "got some starvings" on cold, wet nights. "He nearly always had his head out, looking where he was going, and he'd get cold. After a while, though, he got used to it." Drivers were invariably known by their nicknames. Carlisle men included Big Bass, Old Bulldog and Cuckoo Law – the last named being unlucky when the fire blew back in Stainforth Tunnel and he was so badly burned he died. Dirty Dick was always "mucked up".

Special respect was shown to Holbeck men. Or so they liked to think. The Holbeck shed at Leeds was concerned with the passenger side of the railway. "Holbeck men got the best of the engines and the best of the coal. They'd go by with their noses in the air. We used to call coaches 'mahoganies' though they were only painted with the wood grain. 'He's on mahoganies,' we'd say as a Holbeck train went by." There was a distinct difference between passenger and goods drivers on pay-day. When a goods driver was on 5s.6d a day, a driver on passenger work got the top rate of £7 a week.

Every type of locomotive had to be fired in a special way. The fire was built according to the shape of the firebox. "For Derby 3s and 4s it was 'thick under the door, level to your mouthpiece, almost razor thin at the front'." A Compound firebox was 11ft long and had to be fed through "a narrow little hole". When at night a perspiring fireman on the up-line saw The Star of Bethlehem, his name for the glowing signal at Aisgill, he knew that his spell of really hard effort was almost over. Helm Wind, which was brewed up about High Cup Nick and raged along the East Fellside, was known to pluck coal from the fireman's shovel. He had to wait until the train entered a cutting before he could replenish the fire. A Carlisle man who began work on the railway at Durranhill depot in 1917 when he was 15 years old told the author that his first "firing" job was with Bob Newbould. Bob, a main line driver, was aged 73.

When a fireman was not shovelling, he'd sweep the footplate "to keep the muck down". A fireman was never still

Above: **Two fascinating views of the long-gone water troughs that were located just to the south of Garsdale station. The water tank feeding the troughs held 43,000 gallons and was steam-heated in winter to avoid freezing up.**
Below: **Station staff at Hawes Junction (Garsdale) taken no later than 1907. Third from left, Thomas Addy, was transferred to Addingham soon after.** Courtesy of Denise Tattersall, granddaughter of Thomas Addy

– "wiping down, bending down, sweeping out." At the Garsdale water trough, the driver would bark: "OK, gerrit in." He was referring to the water-scoop. It must be lowered right down, then given a half turn back. "I'd have my eyes on the water gauge. As soon as it was showing three-quarters full I'd start pulling the scoop out. Some drivers complained I could have got more water. If it overflowed, they were just as ratty. There was too much bloody water. I couldn't win!"

The celebrated Garsdale water-troughs gave many footplate men a soaking if the scoop from their locomotives did not encounter the trough at the right time or depth. "If you didn't get it right, water flooded into the cab and soaked the crew – that is, if the troughs were working!" It was said they were frozen over for three months in winter, dry for three months in summer and clogged with leaves for the three autumn months, "leaving only spring as the time when there was any water to be had."

A fireman trained in the York area who served for a time on the Settle-Carlisle worried the veteran driver of a freight train by keeping a low fire. As the train passed 200ft chimney of the

Left: **A study of a railwayman in Midland days at Hellifield.**
Above: **Victorian stationmaster at Settle, Benny Ash, walks under the arch close to the station.**

Hoffman kiln at Craven Quarry, the driver pointed to the chimney and quietly remarked that in next to no time the train would be at Aisgill – at the same elevation as the chimney top. The fireman looked again, then shovelled furiously.

David Tibbetts of Carlisle recalled when he "fired" on the old Midland route to Aisgill. It was in the early part of the Second World War. The knocker-up arrived at his home with a note to say that he must "book on" at 12.03 a.m. to help pilot the Midnight Express up to Aisgill. His driver that night was Big Bass Telford, a huge and kind-hearted man. Bass looked at young David and asked: "Have you ever bin on one of these before?" David shook his head. At this Bass said: "Well, stand over there – out o't'road – and hang on. Just keep an eye open. If you see a yellow signal, shout to me."

And off they set, with David hanging on for grim death and Big Bass shovelling coal and also driving. David recalled: "I was petrified. It was my first experience of the railway and it was black dark. The loco was a Midland type passenger engine, with no doors. I remember seeing the dawn, about

three or four o'clock in the morning, as we returned to Carlisle." By now, Bass was allowing the young man to do the firing. "It's your turn," he had said. David was feeling extremely pleased at the thought of having helped to pilot a Thames-Clyde express on its nocturnal dash across the fells.

Guards

During the Second World War, the driver of a train heading north from Hellifield felt uneasy and suspected that the guard in his van had forgotten to release the brake fully. He stopped at Settle, explaining that he wanted to take on water. The fireman went back to the van, where he found a young guard who had trained in the York area. The brake was indeed the cause of the trouble. The guard confessed he knew little about the Settle-Carlisle and was accustomed to level going. When asked how he knew whether he was going uphill or downhill, he produced some marbles. When in doubt he tossed them on the floor and took note of which way they rolled.

A Hellifield man who became a guard during the Second World War rejoiced because his railway career, like those of many others, had been blighted by the years of industrial depression. Before moving to Hellifield he had been a ticket collector at Heysham in 1932 and, for four years, a temporary guard at Colne. He retired after 43 years service with a railway pension of half-a-guinea a week. He might have "stopped on" but after 43 years "I'd had enough." He kept a railway whistle as a sole tangible link with his railway service. His pride at having worked on the Settle-Carlisle endured.

Signalmen

Signal boxes were built to the standard Midland pattern. The Settle-Carlisle was fitted with block signalling equipment and interlocking points and levers. Wires to the distant signals were connected with devices that took up the slack if they expanded. The Victorian signalmen used electrical instruments showing not only the position of the distant signals but whether or not the lamps were functioning.

In the beginning trains were sent forwards, one after another, on a simple "time interval" basis. A lapse of ten minutes might be allowed. Inevitably there were crashes. The Midland, which was a leader in safety matters, developed the rotary block instruments that protected trains in section between signal boxes. There was a three-position indicator panel with "Line Blocked", "Line Clear" and "Train on Line" displays. A rotating lever that was capable of being moved round through 360 degrees in the three named stages controlled these positions. Only on the completion of this operation might the next train be allowed through the system.

Alfred Sutton, a Leeds man, became employed by the Midland in 1883 and moved to Hawes Junction in 1890. There were then two signal boxes, namely North and South. They were replaced in 1910 by the present structure. A conscientious signalman, grossly overworked, he achieved celebrity in 1910 because of a lapse of concentration towards the end of a busy shift at Garsdale, which was then known as Hawes Junction. By forgetting about two light engines that awaited a clear signal to travel north, and accepting into his section the Scots express, he caused a collision in which there was a heavy death toll. On another occasion, Alfred was in the signal box when a strong wind took told of a locomotive on the turntable

and spun it uncontrollably – until material was shovelled into the turntable pit.

Armathwaite signal box, when built by the Midland in 1899 from prefabricated sections to a standard design, was given extra height so that the signalman could view the goods yard when the refuge siding in front of the box was occupied. The box was closed on 15 January, 1983, after being operated on an "as required" basis for several years. A signal box controlling

The first signal box at Blea Moor which was built in 1892. This was sited on the 'down' side of the line and was replaced in 1941 by the new structure you see today, but relocated to the 'up' side. It was a very remote location with several railwaymen's cottages, a water tank house and various sidings.

traffic in the sidings at Settle closed on 1st May, 1984, and was moved during a "night possession" in the summer of 1996 for about 100 yards to a position in the station yard. It is "open to view" at prescribed times. The box dates from 1891. With it are preserved a 20-lever tumbler frame.

Left: **The interior of Ais Gill signal box. This box was demolished and re-erected at the Midland Railway Centre, Derbyshire.** Above: **Staff pose alongside Crosby Garrett's signal box. It was built in 1899 and lasted until 1967.**
Below left: **Jimmy Richardson was signalman at Culgaith for many years.** Below right: **Dent station signal box.**

Signal boxes

Left: **The signal box at Horton-in-Ribblesdale was responsible not only for through traffic but for mineral trains using the limestone quarry opposite the box.**

Below left: **Blea Moor signal box as it is today on the 'up' side of the main line and close to the path leading to Whernside seen snow-covered in the background.**

Below right: **Selside signal box was roughly half-way between Horton and Ribblehead station. During the Second World War it was famous for having several women operating the signals.**

Above: **Garsdale's signal box is larger than most of the others on the line. Having 40 levers, the 30-foot long structure looked after the main line, sidings and Hawes branch line trains. It superseded two smaller signal boxes at the north and south ends of the station in 1910. It was from this signal box (then known as Hawes Junction) that the unfortunate mistakes were made in 1910 and 1913 which caused two fatal accidents. The signal box was taken out of use in 1983 but re-instated in the 1990s as part of the re-generation of the line.**

Left: **Settle station signal box was located close to the goods shed at the southern end of the station. It had 20 levers and controlled busy goods sidings and main line trains.**

All was not lost when Settle signal box closed in 1984. It lay in a derelict condition until 1996 when the Friends of Settle-Carlisle Line volunteers moved it to a point closer to the station and restored it to its former glory. Roger Hardingham

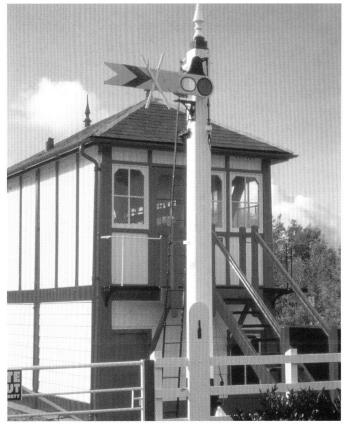

Stations

Obsessed with a desire to have a fast line to Scotland, the Midland concentrated on laying the permanent way. Stations could come later. In the beginning, the Settle-Carlisle was served by 19 stations. The 20th was built at Hawes. Despite its cash problems, the Midland built substantially and in a style that became known as Midland Gothic. By and large, the stone used for facing the stations reflected local geology. Settle was built of freestone. Further up the dale the native limestone was the building material. In Edenvale, red sandstone – which outcrops widely in that area - gave the stations a glowing rose-red aspect on sunny days. The company's architects produced the three standard designs that were categorised as small, medium or large, depending on their passenger status. The basic design was of twin pavilions, separated by a glazed front port.

Steeply pitched roofs made allowance for the extremes of local weather. Such a deep roof was to offer storage space for documents. Bundles of yellowing forms and cashbooks, now of great historical interest, have been recovered from station lofts. Notable features of Settle-Carlisle stations are the fretted bargeboards and trefoil panels on the gables. The larger stations consisted of a complex that included sidings, goods shed and cattle pens. All the stations except Culgaith were provided with flagged platforms. Culgaith was almost an afterthought. The company was short of funds and its

platforms were made of wood. (This station has an adjacent level crossing, the gates being operated by a lever in a nearby signal box).

Hellifield, a few miles south of Settle Junction, was a sprawling station, as befitted its status as a junction with the Lancashire and Yorkshire Railway (Lanky). On to a small village was grafted a range of Victorian villages. The community was shift-conscious, with railwaymen going to work or returning from it by night as well as day. The knocker-up made his doleful rounds, rapping on doors in the well small hours and shouting, "Double-head to Carlisle" or "Relief to Manchester". If he added to his message "…and lodge" it meant that someone would spend a night away from home. A guard whose train encountered snowdrifts at Aisgill returned to Hellifield twenty-one chilling hours later. The crews of the snowploughs quartered at Hellifield worked exceptionally long hours.

A man who presided over a bookstall run by W H Smith at Hellifield had begun work aged 13, his wage being 2s.6d a week. In summer, two boys were employed by the manager, one to deliver newspapers and magazines in the village and the other to carry a basket full of periodicals to the passengers on trains that had stopped for a few minutes. A manageress, three waitresses, a cook and

cellarman staffed the refreshment room. Luncheon baskets were available to passengers. A boy who began work at 7 a.m. had to haul a large four-wheeled barrow along the platforms to collect dirty trays and pots, which were then washed up, using a large bath.

At Settle, vast quantities of material were tipped to create the station and its capacious yard. Perched high above the valley, Settle is notable as a viewpoint. The eye of an intending passenger ranges across North Ribblesdale to a knoll on which stands the domed chapel of Giggleswick School. The station, complete with goods yard and shed, was built of Bradford stone. What began as the ladies waiting room, complete with a fireplace surround of dark fossilised limestone known as Dent marble, became the stationmaster's office. In fairly recent times, there was high office furniture of the Bob Cratchett type. Hissing gas jets provided lighting. The tank house and water tower survive. In the days of steam traction, a 200-gallon tank, fed by water that flowed down a lineside channel from Stainforth, served two water cranes and the station toilets.

Opposite page: **The station at Horton-in-Ribblesdale was a standard Midland Railway No. 3 small type of stone-built structure. Well-known for its best-kept station status in the 1950s.**
Right: **Hellifield is not on the Settle-Carlisle line proper, but a few miles south of Settle junction. Beautifully restored using many grants, this vast station is a unique example.** Roger Hardingham

Above: **The southern laylout at Settle in the early 1960s. The siding, water crane, station lamps, goods shed and signal box are all on view.** Below: **An invention of Stationmaster James Taylor at Settle which he copied from his days at Horton.**

Settle

Two views of Settle station yard taken in the run-down years of the 1970s.

Top: The goods shed and signal box after the sidings had been removed from the site. The goods shed was demolished and the site today plays host to a set of small industrial units. The signal box survives today in a fully restored condition closer to the railway station itself.

Below: Redundant tank house and other outbuildings. The former exists today and is a rare example and is now a listed building.

Left: **The platforms at Garsdale looking south showing the double-tracked main line and tank house.**

Below: **England's highest main line station. Dent station sits on a ledge on the side of the fell. At 1,100 feet above sea level, Dent catches all weathers and in winter was protected by snow fences made from wooden sleepers in an attempt to stop snow covering the line. Most stations along the line now have heritage lighting courtesy of supporting organisations.**

The hillside nature of the Settle-Carlisle line is evident at Horton-in-Ribblesdale. The station has a steep approach road and appears to stand on a ledge. In its heyday, the stationmaster had oversight of the goods traffic emanating from Beecroft Quarry. Ribblehead was also a social centre in the sense that religious services were held in the waiting room, where a harmonium was kept to accompany the hymn-singing. Ribblehead was also a weather-recording station – one of a chain that fed information to the RAF at Leeming. The stationmaster was trained in meteorology and received an extra £1 a week for attending to the hourly reports of the weather. A tall mast supported the rotating cups of the anemometer. With regard to the cloud layer, the known height of Whernside, 2,414ft, was helpful. Otherwise a hydrogen-filled balloon was sent aloft and its progress to the cloud being timed and the height assessed. A rain gauge was introduced in 1954, which was a notoriously wet year, 110 inches of rain being recorded.

Dent station, at an elevation of 1,100ft, is the highest station of any English mainline rail system. The station had not been built when the Settle-Carlisle opened for regular passenger traffic in May, 1876. There were differences of opinion about where it should be placed. Some preferred a site to the south, at Dent Head. In its present position, perched high on the fell, it looks improbable, especially as the winding road to it climbs 450ft in little more than half a mile, the gradient being 1 in 5. The stationmaster's house, for long privately owned, is situated at a point slightly higher than the station and was provided in Midland days with double-glazing, not of the modern type but two windows, set a few inches apart. At Dent, coal traffic was important (most families had hitherto burnt peat).

Garsdale, formerly Hawes Junction, is three miles from any sizeable community. It had a life of its own. Up to the closure of the Hawes branch, this was the only true junction station on the Settle-Carlisle. In the halcyon days before the 1914-18 war, the station saw considerable activity. Almost every train was double-headed and the pilots were detached here, to be turned before returning as light engines to Hellifield or Carlisle. It was nothing unusual for a signalman to be handling over half a dozen light engines. The company had hoped to establish an engine shed for two dozen locomotives. Thirty cottages were to be constructed for the employees. The shed scheme was abandoned when finances were cramped during the closing stages of the line's construction. Garsdale did eventually acquire a small engine shed. It was used by the North-Eastern Railway, which usually worked the service to Hawes. The shed was burnt down in 1917, being rebuilt but closed down in 1939. The Hawes service closed in 1959 and the track was lifted. If a ghostly train were to be seen on a moonlit night, it will surely be that of Bonnyface, the Bradford-Hawes train, which was put on Garsdale's turntable and travelled tender first to Hawes, returning at 4.25 p.m. It is said to have been nicknamed Bonnyface after a particularly ugly permanent way inspector who spent half the journey with his head and shoulders out of a carriage window, checking on the work.

Old-timers recalled when the Methodist chapel near the Moorcock viaduct was packed, especially for evangelical services, which were spread over a week. In fairly recent times, services were held in the waiting room and the hymn-singing had accompaniment by a harmonium. Gone is the 200-volume library, a gift of a thoughtful lady passenger. A visitor no longer sees the 80,000-gallon tank which in steam days

The turntable at Garsdale had a stockade built around it to protect it from high winds. LMS numbered tank engine No. 10899 is in the process of being turned. Legend has it that a locomotive spun out of control on this turntable during high winds and was only stopped after sand was poured into the pit. The turntable survives today at the preserved Keighley & Worth Valley Railway at Keighley station.

supplied water for thirsty locomotives. The Tank House was from the 1930s until the coming of television a centre for domino and whist drives, potato pie suppers, concerts, even dances.

With the decline and eventual end of piloting, the turntable became obsolete and was removed several years before the end of steam haulage. People still recalled a wild night when an engine that was being turned was caught broadside by the wind and spun out-of-control. Eventually, sand was poured into the well of the turntable as a method of braking. Henceforth, the turntable was surrounded by a stockade to cheat the wind. A mile or two down the line, nature could still re-assert itself. A woman living in a cottage near Aisgill who hung her washing on open ground almost trod on a peewit's nest.

Hawes had a curious frontier flavour, for although the Midland owned the station it was staffed by the North-Eastern, who also worked most of the trains through to Garsdale. Separate accounts were kept for each company. During its heyday, thousands of flagstones, slates and building stones were consigned from Wensleydale quarries by rail. Goods services were withdrawn from the Wensleydale

Kirkby Stephen station is one of three now looked after by the Settle-Carlisle Railway Trust. Ribblehead and Horton-in-Ribblesdale are the others. This station was once known as Kirkby Stephen West because just down the hill towards the town itself, was Kirkby Stephen East. This latter station is being restored for use as part of the Eden Valley Railway project. The station above is now open again for business and a self catering apartment can be rented.

Courtesy of Andrew Griffiths, imagerail.com

branch in 1964; the metals were lifted. In 1884, a station was proposed for Mallerstang and the Midland agreed to provide it if the dalesfolk would built an approach road at a cost of £2,200. Lord Hothfield offered land for the site but the necessary money could not be found.

The longest run between two stations used to be that between Garsdale and Kirkby Stephen, the last-named being 1 ½ miles from the town centre. It was once named Kirkby Stephen and Ravenstonedale, which was at a much greater distance. In the Eden Valley, the station at Crosby Garrett was built in a cutting that was 55ft deep. Appleby's platforms have an exceptional length, one of them extending to 200 yards. Water to replenish the locomotives was pumped for 140ft from the Eden to a tank at the station. Culgaith station was unusual in having a level crossing at the end of the platform, this being the first level crossing on the line.

At Langwathby, where the service of local stopping trains ended in 1970, the conversion of the main building into a restaurant called Brief Encounter was completed in April, 1996.

The Citadel station at Carlisle, opened in 1847, was built of Yorkshire stone. A Victorian structure on the grand scale it had the flavour of Tudor days in the size and style of fireplaces set in the refreshment room. In the stationmaster's office were the crests of the original private companies, joined later by those of the LMS and British Railways. When the Midland came to town, it was the seventh to make use of the joint station.

Above **Appleby is the second busiest station on the line after Settle. The building is the large type as at Settle and Kirkby Stephen and was constructed out of brick and local stone. The station was the only one on the line which provided a passenger footbridge. Today, Settle and Kirkby Stephen have been provided with these. There were two stations at Appleby - 'West' (the one pictured) and 'East'. The East station closed in 1962 following closure of the North Eastern route.**

Right: End of a 72-mile journey at Carlisle Citadel station. Viewed in 1979, an electric service on the West Coast Main Line is in one of the main platforms. Settle-Carlisle trains use the bay platform on the right-hand side. People living in this area call the line 'the Carlisle-Settle' and not the Settle-Carlisle!

Above: **The entrance to Settle station in the 1960s. The neat gardens and gated driveway show a great pride in the station. The tank house is the large building in the right background.** Opposite page: **Railway workers attend to the track at Settle station.**

Stationmasters

With their smart uniforms and air of considerable authority, the Settle-Carlisle stationmasters were much respected. It was a general view that they just pottered about, having plenty of staff to do the varied jobs. Benny Ash, for many years stationmaster at Settle, would "let his men know he was boss, striding up and down the platform when a train was in – and then nipping off to the Golden Lion for a whisky."

When Douglas Cobb was stationmaster at Garsdale in 1953, he created a platform garden. The gardening tradition was nowhere better demonstrated than at Horton-in-Ribblesdale, and later at Settle, when the stationmaster was Jim Taylor. A

former stationmaster at Dent attempted to grow flowers and vegetables at an elevation of 1,155ft. He also kept an eye on the line for trespassing sheep and told the author: "Any sheep that is knocked down by a train is always the best in the flock. There's never a bad one among them."

Bill Sharpe, stationmaster at Ribblehead, also ran the local weather station. After working as a farm man, he entered railway service in 1949. His career reflected the vagaries of the Settle-Carlisle. He was porter, signalman, stationmaster, area assistant manager (for a month) and then became relief signalman. The aforementioned James (Jim) Taylor began his Settle-Carlisle service in 1947, not long after the line had been blotted out by big snowfalls. He became stationmaster at

James Taylor, stationmaster at Settle, receives an award for the best-kept station. Above right: **Another of his creations at Horton-in-Ribblesdale.**

Horton-in-Ribblesdale and turned a bleak little station into one that became renowned for its floral displays. He also attended to goods traffic connected with a huge limestone quarry.. A favourite tale was of the farmer who, finding a dead sheep, threw it over a wall on to railway property, just as some permanent way men were passing, unseen to the farmer, who was startled when the sheep was thrown back over the wall.

In the late 1950s, Jim Taylor moved to Settle and, once again, devoted much of his spare time to beautifying the platforms with beds of flowers. Officially, he persuaded authority to allow more passenger trains to stop at Settle, which led to a 40% increase in local takings.

Workforce

Generations of dedicated railwayfolk, living sparsely in remote areas, have ensured the smooth operation of the Settle-Carlisle. They were to remember in particular the extremes of climate. Station staff clambered up signals to replenish the fuel. Maintenance gangs were buffeted by the wind and drenched by rain as they attended to the permanent way. Masons were chilled on the viaducts. The tunnel gangs emerged from their shifts looking like miners. It needed a special form of dedication to be on shift duty at a remote signal box such as Blea Moor.

Railway work was considered secure. A man was carefully vetted. He had a temporary appointment for about two years before being given a permanent position. The temporary man received 2s or so more than the regular employees. In the 1930s, a platelayer was given accommodation in one of the cottages in Salt Lake. He earned 31s.9d with stoppages, which was an average wage for the district. The quarryman earned a bit more. Of the wage, the platelayer paid 5s.4d in rent.

John Mason, who was employed at Hawes station for 48 years, retiring in 1948, remembered an instruction in the railway rule book that a servant should be "prompt, civil and obliging." It was an instruction to which he responded when

Garsdale in the 1960s. A local pick-up goods operation underway with a Standard class locomotive shunting wagons around the 'up' and 'down' lines in the station.

dealing with people, not only at work but in his daily life. Incidentally, he had begun work at 15s a week; he returned as porter-signalman with a wage of £5.2s a week.

A newly-appointed porter at Little Salkeld was permitted to catch a train and start work at Lazonby at 8 a.m. The stationmaster introduced him to his work, as listed on some paper that was attached to the back of a cupboard door. There were several lists, one for cattle dock man and another for those employed in the goods shed. The longest list – "it was as long as my arm" – applied to the new porter. The stationmaster said they were simple jobs. The porter told his parents: "Simple they may be – but there are an awful lot of them."

A junior porter was at the "beck and call" of everyone. "Hey, son, I've forgotten my dinner. Nip out for two pies," someone would shout. And the porter had to oblige. At Newbiggin station, during the Second World War, the junior porter visited the gypsum mine to label the wagons. "It wasn't much I was paid. I finished up, after 16 years, with £6.10s. That was my top wage."

The Chapel-le-Dale postman, who operated on foot, delivered letters for cottages at Blea Moor. The family shopping was carried out in Settle. Groceries were delivered to Ribblehead station once a month. From here the groceries were transported to Blea Moor by the stopping freight train.

Left: **A lineside gang at work on a section of the track. Many hundreds of workers would be kept employed along the whole route between Settle junction and Carlisle looking after the track and signalling equipment.**

Below: **The last stationmaster at Ribblehead, William (Bill) Sharpe. His son Geoffrey is seen with him. He was a porter there. Bill would send weather information from Ribblehead in coded messages to the Air Ministry to be included in the national picture.**

Harry Cox, who worked on the line before the First World War recalled the type of cabin built by men engaged in viaduct or tunnel work; it was entirely home-made from such materials as railway sleepers. Men even made their own seats. The foreman would knock up a rough cupboard in which he could keep his papers. The fireplace extended into the room and was adorned by a metal plate on which food was warmed. The fireman allowed a man to go to the cabin an hour before "bait" time to prepare the food, which was commonly "half a collop of bacon and a couple of eggs."

Passengers

When the Midland had its direct, all-weather route to Scotland for which it had yearned, its rivals on the east and west coast lines strove to remain competitive by revising their services and reducing their fares. Trains on the Lancaster-Carlisle were accelerated. The new line's real importance was as a direct and independent connection with the systems of two Scottish companies, these being the Glasgow and South-Western and the North British. The Midland had also shrugged off the rent of between £70,000 and £80,000 a year it paid for running powers on the Lancaster-Carlisle.

The Midland made a fuss of its passengers. Its rivals thought this was almost to the point of benevolence. Upholstered carriages were available to third-class passengers and, the carriages being unheated, foot-warmers were

Unexpected passenger traffic appeared during the First World War. Local young men were conscripted to the services and these here were to depart from Settle station for a very uncertain future.

available at stations. There was also, for a short time on the Settle-Carlisle, de luxe travel. During a visit to America in 1872, James Allport met George M Pullman, whose Palace Car Company made an impact in the New World with large, open, luxurious carriages, heated by a closed circuit of hot-water pipes, attached to a boiler lit by kerosene.

Pullman was invited to meet the Midland shareholders and declared that he could run coaches "equal to a first-class hotel." His claim being put to the test, difficulties arose in matching an American system to the British, not least with regard to bogies and couplings. The cars were built in Detroit, dismantled for transhipment to Derby and re-built by the Pullman Company in a large shed constructed for the purpose. The first of the cars, ready for use in January, 1874, were incorporated in the day and night expresses operating from St Pancras to Glasgow and Edinburgh. When the Settle-Carlisle was opened, therefore, the Midland had been operating Pullmans for more than a year.

Two Pullman drawing room cars (Juno and Britannia) were attached to the first train that operated between London and Glasgow by way of the Settle-Carlisle. The first express train from Edinburgh and the North consisted of eight vehicles, these being two Pullman cars, three novel long carriages constructed on the bogie principle and three composite brake carriages. The Pullman coaches were undoubtedly luxurious but, not being divided into compartments, they were draughty and, more to the point with Victorian travellers, lacked the privacy afforded by coaches that were compartmentalised. Within a short time, these brash American intruders were removed from use on Settle-Carlisle line.

Dining cars came into use in 1892. Under an old arrangement, a cold luncheon basket might be purchased at Hellifield for a charge of 3s. The type of food available to rail-users was mouth-watering. It included chicken with ham or tongue, salad, cheese, butter, half bottle of burgundy, claret, stout, apollinaris or a bottle of aerated water. A roaring coal

Above: **A reminder of Pullman Car traffic over the line in the early 20th century. This example survived at Hellifield as an office for many years. A garden in front befitting a Pullman.**
Below: **A major source of goods traffic was from the quarry at Horton-in-Ribblesdale. This scene is from the railway sidings within the quarry.**

During the Great War services were reduced and the Midland took on a careworn appearance. Shortly after the war ended, grouping of railway companies brought the Midland and its former deadly rival, the London and North-Western together as the London, Midland and Scottish Railway. The 1930s saw a return to a service whereby three expresses ran each way daily. The time taken to cover the 309 miles from St Pancras to Carlisle was just over six hours. The morning expresses to and from Glasgow and Edinburgh had the grand titles of Thames-Clyde and Thames-Forth. The Waverley route was closed in January, 1969 and the Thames-Clyde was stripped of its name and, instead of running non-stop from Leeds to Carlisle, called at Skipton, Hellifield, Settle and Appleby. In 1977 Nottingham not London became the starting point for expresses that traversed the Settle-Carlisle.

Local services with withdrawn from the old Midland route to Scotland on 5th May, 1970, when all stations on the line except Settle and Appleby were closed. The Hawes branch was shut in 1959 and the track was subsequently lifted. The Settle-Carlisle had the occasional burst of activity as a diversion route on Sundays when engineering work led to the temporary closure of the Lancaster-Carlisle line over Shap. Dalesrail provided a monthly weekend service during the tourist season and on special occasions.

fire heated the refreshment room at Hellifield. The ale was of such quality that men living locally called for their end-of-the-day pints.

Passenger traffic on the Settle-Carlisle reached its zenith just before the Great War clouded the Edwardian sunset and, in the longer term, radically altered the social structure of the country. Each day, three expresses left St Pancras to use the Settle-Carlisle, having through carriages for both Glasgow and Edinburgh. A night express from St Pancras departed at 9-30 with sleeping cars for Glasgow, Edinburgh, Dundee, Aberdeen, Perth and (in summer) for Inverness. It divided at Leeds. Here were attached carriages from Bristol. Portions from Liverpool and Manchester were added at Hellifield. Night trains connected the Midland with Glasgow and Stranraer, enabling passengers to use the shortest sea route to Ireland.

Freight

The Midland's main objective in building the Settle-Carlisle was to speed goods from England to Scotland. Local traffic was of lesser importance. The Midland recovered some of its outlay even before the Settle-Carlisle was completed. With the southern part ready, they could transport limestone from Craven Quarry at Langcliffe to the "iron districts" near Bradford. Lime was also needed for plastering, fluxing, bleaching and for sweetening sour land. Eventually, sidings at Craven Quarry at Langcliffe ran on either side of an immense Hoffman Kiln, devised by a German for continuous burning. Though mainly used elsewhere for brick-making, the Hoffman was suitable for burning limestone.

The kiln had two long sides connected by curved ends. Two fires fed by coal following each other round. In advance of fire, a chamber was stacked with blocks of lime and sealed off. The fire, stimulated by draughts and fed by coal from above, burnt the lime, which had been stacked leaving appropriate gaps. When the fire had passed, the chamber was opened up and the lime wheel-barrowed on planks into waiting railway wagons. Being labour intensive, its days were numbered. John Delaney, sensing the importance of the railway to the commercial life of the area, opened up Beecroft quarry at Horton-in-Ribblesdale and had sidings installed. The railway brought him coal and took away his lime. He had the distinction of owning wagons on which the name Delaney was emblazoned.

The large limestone quarry at Langcliffe near Settle. The Hoffman kiln can be clearly seen on the left in this aerial view.

Left: **The internal siding associated with the quarry at Foredale near Helwith Bridge. Stone would come down from this quarry for transport out via the main line.**

Below: **The pick-up goods at Blea Moor in the 1960s.**

The start of regular goods traffic in 1876 led to the routing of nine trains each way per day. It was not uncommon for tarpaulins to be ripped off wagons at Ribblehead and be blown a mile or so away, a windfall in a literal sense for any farmer short of stock sheets. There were regular trains for cattle and sheep. The Settle-Carlisle was soon handling livestock transferred to the line by the two associated Scottish companies. In 1876, a vast new goods station had been built at Carlisle. It was said to cover 80 acres and to be complete with engine sheds, goods warehouses and cattle docks. In due course, loops would be laid down at Blea Moor to allow for the unimpeded passage of express passenger trains. Goods trains could be shunted off the main line.

James Pratt, of Hawes, was a cattle dealer with strong Scottish connections. Local farmers collected the stock from the station or employed a drover like Tommy

Byker of Garsdale. The cattle usually arrived on a late train. It was not unknown for Tommy to walk them through the night. All the surplus farmstock went by rail. A special train left Hawes on Monday evenings. When, in October, the sheep sales took place, more specials were required. Dalesfolk converted their surplus milk into butter or cheese and sold them locally. A number, having contacts with milkmen in towns, transported milk kits in horse-drawn floats to the nearest station. There was no guarantee that the urban dealer would pay his bills and Dales farmers came close to cheering when, in the 1930s, the Milk Marketing Board was established and they had a guaranteed market.

Anhydrite workings were opened south of Cumwhinton. Long Meg gave her name to a gypsum mine. The rock was transported by rail to Widnes. Railway sidings were installed at Long Meg and during the course of the next two decades about two million tons of "blue cobble" passed over the Settle-Carlisle. In 1993 the first regular freight flow to use the line since its reprieve from closure in 1989 began running. The service, which has continued to the present day, carries gypsum from Drax Power Station to the plaster board factory at Kirkby Thore in the Eden Valley. In recent years, the heavily-laden freights had to cope not only with the 1 in 100 gradient of the Long Drag but with leaves falling on to the tracks from tree-lined cuttings. Slippery conditions caused by leaf-mulch were a problem until many lineside trees were felled and a special train devised to clean the rails.

The signal box at Long Meg was brought into use in 1955. The extensive sidings here were extremely busy with transport of the mineral anhydrite. The complex was closed in 1975.

Speed Trials

The Settle-Carlisle having a rigorous route and continuous gradient, might have been especially made for trials and experiments. A new type of sanding gear was tried out in 1886 and as a result the Midland began to use steam instead of compressed air for sanding purposes. When grouping had taken place, locomotives of three of the old companies were pitted against each other. These were a London and North-Western Prince of Wales 4-6-0, a Caledonian 2-cylinder simple 4-4-0 and a Midland Compound. An outcome of the test was that the Midland constructed more Compounds.

When the railways were nationalised, a range of locomotives was extensively tested on the route. Of the diesel stock, the Class 45 would be the mainstay for many years. The Class 47 was used on diverted expresses and became standard haulage for Glasgow-bound passenger trains. The Class 45 was retained on freight trains.

Snowtime

Appearing in the LMS General Appendix was a caution that hardly needed to be expressed in words. It was that "stationmasters and signalmen between Hellifield and Carlisle must carefully watch the weather during the winter months." From Midland days, the Pennine winter was taken seriously enough for snowploughs to be positioned at Hellifield. The snow fences made of upreared sleepers and positioned above deep cuttings at Dent were an attempt by puny man to prevent drifting snow from clogging the line.

A blizzard in 1933 closed the line for almost a week. The stove pipe was the only visible feature of the signal box at Mallerstang which had been enveloped by a huge drift. A submerged locomotive was found when a snow-digger on a drift stuck a tentative spade into a metal cylinder. It was the engine's chimney. In 1963, the Edinburgh-London sleeper was stranded in a drift. The trouble arose at about 3 a.m. on 20 January. The drift had formed to the south of Rise Hill Tunnel. Happily, it was possible to transfer the passengers to the back three coaches, which – with the line cleared – were worked back to Carlisle in a blizzard, the engine running tender-first.

Snow arrives in the Pennines during the winter of 1947 and affects the Settle-Carlisle line in a dramatic way. After filling wagons with snow, workmen empty the contents over the side of a viaduct in Dentdale.

Two scenes here show how deep the snow was in the Dent area. The 'up' station platform and waiting shelter is somewhere beneath the drift of snow on the left!

No regular trains passed through Dent station for five days. Cornices reared elegantly but dangerously over 20ft high drifts at the edge of the cutting. Passengers in a marooned sleeping car train had to be rescued. A stone billet was available for men having a respite from snow-clearing duty. Food for the snow-clearers was sent from the railway refreshment room at Preston.

The worst spell of wintry weather in living memory occurred in 1947, when the Settle-Carlisle was closed for eight weeks. The trouble arose not so much from the amount of snow but because it was drifted by a continuing fierce wind and, compacted, turned into ice. Dent station almost vanished from sight, the cutting being blocked by banks of snow crusted with ice that derailed a plough to which two locomotives were attached. Isolated families living near the line received groceries by courtesy of the crew of a light engine and brake. Clearing the track involved a special force of 500

A snow-covered platform at Ribblehead station. The drifts have virtually reached the roof. The 'down' line has been cleared.

men, including soldiers and German prisoners-of-war, some of whom rebelled in the harsh conditions, throwing their shovels over a viaduct.

Ernest Jarvis, of Skipton, the driver of a steam locomotive, recalled a protracted journey in the winter of 1947. "We signed on to work the 5-45 p.m. from Skipton to Garsdale, where we had to pick up a train. It started to snow. I'd only half a tank of water, but it was enough to take me to Blea Moor, where I could fill up. They stopped me at Ribblehead. The 'Leeds man' was coming up behind and he hadn't any water. I said: 'Neither have I, owd lad.' They said: 'It saves a block.' I said: 'I don't care what it's going to save, in t'long run it's going to lose.'

"I hadn't to go until the Leeds man came. So he came. According to his water gauge, he'd more water than I had. Remember, I set off from Skipton with half a tank and that was at 5-45 p.m. Now it was eight o'clock the next morning. It had taken some time, and I'd climbed up half a dozen posts on purpose to see whether pegs were up or not! When we got to Garsdale eventually, they dug us out of snow and let us go across to let this Leeds man come before us. They couldn't get points up so they had to let us go first.

"Our train – a munitions train from the Hawes branch, was in a lay-by, with a brake at each end. They got facing points up but the trailing points wouldn't come. They'd reckoned that when I trailed through them, they'd shut, squeezing out the snow. We got inside nearly except for four wheels of the engine! In the meantime, the guard had taken the back brake off and was just climbing out of the front brake next to the engine. He shoved us a bit, so they had to let us go. That's when I walked straight off the vans into Mallerstang box. You couldn't see no Mallerstang valley. I asked the signalman how he was going on for a relief and he told me it was his third day at the box. 'How is tha going on for grub then?' 'They're sending it up.' I said: 'Oh, we'll have a share wi' thee.' He said: 'You can have what you like.'

"So we had some sandwiches and a couple of oxo cubes and some snow watter - and that were that! The two snow ploughs from Hellifield were at Kirkby Stephen, moving backards and forrards to fill up with watter. There was no room for two roads. Eventually they came thrusting up. The inspector, Bert Minn, a grand understanding chap, said: 'Na then, how are you going on?' I says: 'In t'muck.' To tell you the truth, the gauge was out. We had 500 gallons more than what the gauge said. The inspector asked me if I'd enough water for Appleby... I said: 'Yes, to tell you the honest gospel truth, if there's nowt on t'road we've enough there for Appleby. Course, we'll have nowt to throw away.'

"So they let us go before the ploughs, on condition we didn't pick up any water at Kirkby Stephen. The Leeds man was well back. Aisgill or somewhere. At Appleby, my fireman went looking for some food. He came back with twelve meat pies in a flour bag (they hadn't t'sense to empty t'flour out of it), a packet of cigarettes, half an ounce of thin twist (for me) and a box of matches. He must have been away for an hour. The signalman shouts: 'Are you about right now?' I said: 'Just about, old lad, but give us time to put a shovel in t'fire-oil and warm up some pies.' I had two pies. The fireman scoffed the rest.

"We landed at the main line, Darranhill. I remember laughing at my fireman, with his black face. Think on, it was mid-day, the day after we'd started. The inspector gave us three cheers. They all cheered. It seems we were the first train to get through from the south for three days. The passenger trains had come over t'Nor'west, by Ingleton. Somebody said: 'Control wants you.' I said: 'They're a bit late in t'day, aren't they?' We were told to book on at Kingmoor, but I didn't want to go there. Last time it happened they were puncturing fish tins to see if there were any fit to eat. We'd go into town, for a wash and brush up, cos we were looking like two chimney

Staff attempt to dig out the pointwork and begin the task of de-frosting the track so that some operations could re-start.

sweeps. Then we'd go to find the most high-class restaurant we could find!

"We heard an express was going from Citadel on the Nor-west line. We got into t'first coach and afore it got to Lowgill I was fast asleep. We signed off at a quarter to six. That wasn't a bad do, was it? Though I've had even worst times down t'pits."

A pair of LMS Class 4Fs equipped with a snow plough. Below is a more modern plough seen on the line. Bob Swallow

Accidents

In the year 1876, when the Midland vigorously began to recoup its expenditure on the Settle-Carlisle, William Betts died from his injuries when he was blown on to the "four foot" near Crosby Garrett in front of a train. Two months later, young George Bryer was struck by the "workmen's" engine between Selside and Salt Lake. He was lifted on to a goods train heading for Settle and died during the short journey. A near escape from disaster occurred inside Blea Moor Tunnel in 1878, an express running into the rear of a slow train that had stalled. Happily, the express managed to lower its speed to about 10 mph at the moment of impact. None of the passengers was seriously injured.

The two most notorious accidents were in 1910 and 1913 on the high-lying stretches between Garsdale and Aisgill. The accident of Christmas Eve, 1910, was especially poignant in view of the time of year. It was also a consequence of negligence on the part of the aforementioned signalman at Garsdale, which was then known as Hawes Junction. It was a day when there were heavy showers of rain on a blustery wind. The signalman was having a busy night. There had been numerous light engines that had piloted expresses up either side of this bleak summit length; they must be turned before returning to Carlisle or Hellifield.

Two light engines that had piloted two up-trains early that day waited for the signal that would permit them to return to Carlisle. The signals were pulled off at 5-30 am, permitting access to the down main line. The signalman forgot their presence as he handled a succession of up trains. The drivers of the light engines did nothing to remind him as at 5-44 am they left the station. The signals came off for a down express, St Pancras and Glasgow, As those engines came off the viaduct at Lunds, the express, which was double-headed, caught them up, ploughing into them at 65 miles an hour.

The carriages of the express being gas-lit, the collision was followed by a fierce blaze, reducing the carriages to a heap of charred wood. Twelve passengers died and nine were injured. The hapless signalman reported to his superiors: "I have wrecked the Scots express." (This accident led to track circuits being installed on main lines at important junctions).

The sad scene near Ais Gill where two accidents in three years occurred with great loss of life.

Above: **An LMS 'Crab' class is re-railed close to an embankment using block and tackle.**
Right: **A derailment at Settle in the early 20th century. The parapet of the arch has been breached by a wagon.**

Less than three years later, on 2nd September, 1913, in the early hours of yet another dark, wet night, a sleeper from Glasgow and Stranraer to St Pancras came to a stand half a mile north of Aisgill summit. An overloaded train, it had run short of steam through poor quality coal. No pilot had been available. Following the sleeper was a night train from Inverness and Edinburgh, the footplate crew of which also in difficulty because of inferior coal. Pre-occupied with trying to get sufficient steam, they over-ran the signals at Mallerstang and collided with the back of the stationary train. As before, fire broke out. Sixteen passengers died and 38 were injured.

On 19th January, 1918, a landslip occurred in Long Meg cutting, between Little Salkeld and Lazonby, immediately ahead of a daytime St Pancras to Glasgow express. The driver had no chance to reduce speed and the train plunged into the soggy clay at a speed of 60 miles an hour, telescoping the two leading coaches. Seven passengers died. A repetition of this tragedy was avoided only because of the vigilance of a driver

passing through the cutting north of Dent Head. He noticed that the ground was bulging ominously and conveyed a warning.

In 1948, a railwayman was killed when a 50-ton breakdown crane that ran away travelled 23 miles from Griseburn to Lazonby. Four years later, 29 passengers were injured when the up Thames-Clyde was derailed at Blea Moor.

A serious accident occurred on 11th January, 1960, when the driver of a 'Britannia' class locomotive working the Glasgow to St Pancras night express stopped at Garsdale to examine his engine but did not notice that both the right hand slide-bars had dropped off. At Settle, the connecting rod finally fell away from the piston and ploughed into the track. A down goods train was derailed and struck the St Pancras train, causing the death of five passengers. In the winter of 1964, a consignment of cars was blown from a train on top of Ribblehead viaduct.

Disaster at Settle junction in 1979. This freight train of Cornish China clay and some Welsh coal derailed at the junction on 2nd May. The huge clearing up process was made all the more difficult due to the clay material. It closed the railway to Carlisle and to Lancaster for a number of days.

Disaster occurred on the last day of January in 1995. Flooding, landslip and a radio blackspot led to a collision between two Sprinters on a remote stretch of track above Mallerstang. A conductor died. Twenty-six passengers were injured. With prolonged, torrential rain causing flooding above rail level in Stainforth cutting, it was decided to stop the southbound 4-26 pm Carlisle to Leeds train at the signalbox on Blea Moor. The train crossed on to the northbound line and began its return journey to Carlisle, where it was planned to transfer passengers to a bus bound for Leeds. The heavy rain weakened a section of embankment above Mallerstang, about one and a-half miles north of Aisgill summit. The affected piece slipped on to the northbound track and derailed the northbound Sprinter, the front coach slewing across the southbound track.

A radio message relating to the incident was sent to Settle Junction signal box, who telephoned York control. The message was relayed to the signal box at Kirkby Stephen. Unhappily, the 5-45 Carlisle to Leeds train had already left Kirkby Stephen and radio contact could not be established, so the driver had no knowledge of the blocked line. All the signalman at Kirkby Stephen could do, fearing an accident, was to call out the emergency services. The obstructing coach was on a bend in the track. Stuart Wilson, the conductor, with great presence of mind, had moved the passengers to the rear. He was the one who died.

Above: **The signal box at Settle Junction which controls both the Carlisle and Lancaster lines. Since this photograph was taken, minor modifications have been made to the exterior.** Roger Hardingham

Above: **Steam cranes from Leeds and Carlisle working to clear the wreckage of the St Blazey-Carlisle freight which derailed at Settle Junction on 2nd May 1979.**

Right: **The China Clay wagons had wooden planked bodies which smashed, leaving the white clay like snow on the ground. Derek Soames, signalman at Settle junction for 23 years until 1995, was not on duty that day but recalled the accident and the aftermath. It is said that some china clay is still to be found on the site to this day!**

War Years

During the 1939-45 war, the locomotives became rough. "Everything became rough," a Skipton driver recalled. "It was hard work on the Drag. Clonk, clonk, clonk." As he went to work in the black-out he stumbled into one of Kit Spensley's horses, which had strayed when someone left the field gate open. "Another night I was wandering along, holding the railing, when I put my right arm round a courting couple."

With the outbreak of war, there was but one passenger service a day from St Pancras to Scotland. When it was north of Leeds, it called at Skipton, Hellifield and Appleby. A train from Leeds, which followed the Scotch Express, stopped at all stations. At Carlisle, it connected with stations in Scotland. The train from Leeds preceded the London train when, as often happened, it ran late. Drivers worked for long periods. One who went on duty on Saturday night did not see his home again until the following Thursday. "I'd worked a train to Carlisle, lodged there, came back to Hellifield, got relieved, went to Carnforth, lodged there...and so on."

The trains became longer and heavier. Some of the viaducts had to be strengthened. Lunds viaduct was concreted in between the spandrels. Armathwaite viaduct was filled in with concrete. A troop train ran into four railwaymen at Settle. "They'd been mending a water main. They didn't hear the train coming – and they died. There were a lot of troop trains." A Hellifield driver, relief on the 10-25 Leeds-Glasgow, clambered on to the footplate and came face to face with a soldier, who told him he had put a "tommy-gun" on the tender. When some prisoners escaped from Shap Well, a signalman on the Settle-Carlisle was among those alerted. It was believed the prisoners were in his area. "If it hadn't been serious, I'd have laughed at the thought of facing some armed Germans with a hand-brush."

The footplate crew did not always know what was in the wagons. The arrival of the Americans at Scottish ports led to the transportation via the Settle-Carlisle of such large objects as tanks and jeeps. The practice of crews riding on their tanks had to be stopped. At home, there were few bridges. On the Settle-Carlisle, bridges were common and decapitation likely.

The signal box at the summit of the line at Ais Gill would see many wartime trains pass through its section. The Settle-Carlisle was a crucial route for the transfer of freight and servicemen during the war years.

Drivers were inclined to give a ride to anyone who'd missed their train or for any believable reason. "Ballast trains and pick-ups were popular."

A Settle-Carlisle signalman coped as well as he could with an eighth of an inch on his pilot light. "You also had your hand-lamp, of course, but during the war this had a great big long shade. It was black as neet but I wasn't to tell to put a leet out if there was danger." The line was busy; the men were happy. Old chaps who had been kept on were "damned thankful" to be working.

With food scarce in town and city, drivers were inclined to stop at signal boxes where they might collect a dozen eggs or a couple of rabbits. One signalman put a note on the door: "Rabbits and Eggs". The driver of one regular train ordered them in advance. A signalman confided in a friend that he was going around the district, buying eggs at 2s.3d and a driver was giving him 4s.6d "with an extra ten bob for myself."

The gradual run-down of services along the Settle-Carlisle resulted in most of the stations closing in May 1970, leaving just Settle and Appleby still in operation.

Above: **A Class 31 diesel hauls a rake of carriages at Culgaith. Like many other stations, Culgaith had lost its passenger services on 4th May 1970.**

Left: **Following the withdrawal of local stopping services in 1970, ambitious supporters decided to try out their own trains to give ramblers and local people the opportunity to travel. Dales Rail began in 1975 and eventually stopped at some of the closed stations. This highly successful approach grew in popularity which eventually helped to save the line from closure.** Ruth Evans collection

A Second Coming

Hopes that the Settle-Carlisle centenary in May, 1975 would be celebrated with steam over the line were not realised. British Railways did allow the Flying Scotsman and LNWR No. 790 Hardwicke to travel from Carnforth to Settle, but they stayed on the siding in Settle yard for the afternoon celebrations. Then, in March 1978, mainline steam was back with a "special" hauled by LNER Green Arrow. The run took place in typical weather – a blizzard.

From 1980, a series of Cumbrian Mountain Expresses were operated with great success. It was the "second coming" of steam to the Settle-Carlisle. In the winter of 1980, a Cumbrian Mountain Express ran on 22nd March. Peter Fox, one of those who excitedly witnessed it, drove up the Lune Valley in a blizzard, having an increasing feeling of madness at having selected Aisgill summit as his first photo-stop. At Aisgill, the sky had cleared of snow. The dispersal of dark clouds meant that Wild Boar Fell was transformed into a dazzling background for railway photography. He was enthralled as a Black Five (No. 5305) conquered the Drag. The combination of a dazzling landscape and a locomotive under steam filled all present with delight and wonder.

The diesel age dawned in the 1960s. Type 4 diesels took charge of expresses in 1963 and local trains became two-car diesel multiple units in 1966.

A Type 4 diesel crosses Ribblehead with one of the final Anglo-Scottish through trains in the early 1980s.

Steam specials started over the Settle-Carlisle line again in 1978, ten years after BR ran the last steam train in Britain. The fact this train ran via the Settle-Carlisle shows how important the route was in the eyes of many. The first train to run by steam again was hauled by 'V2' Green Arrow.

Above: **The National Railway Museum's Stanier Pacific, No. 46229 Duchess of Hamilton, was a regular performer over the line before being entombed at York once more.**

Left: **Possibly the most famous steam locomotive in the world, No. 4472 Flying Scotsman heads a south-bound train at Dent.**

Whilst steam specials brought thousands of people over the line from the 1970s, the structures were decaying and crumbling.
Above: **The waiting shelter at Dent looks very forlorn.**
Left: **Major repair were required on the piers of most viaducts including Ribblehead. Repairs to all of these would take place within a few years.** Below: **Ribblehead station was derelict.**

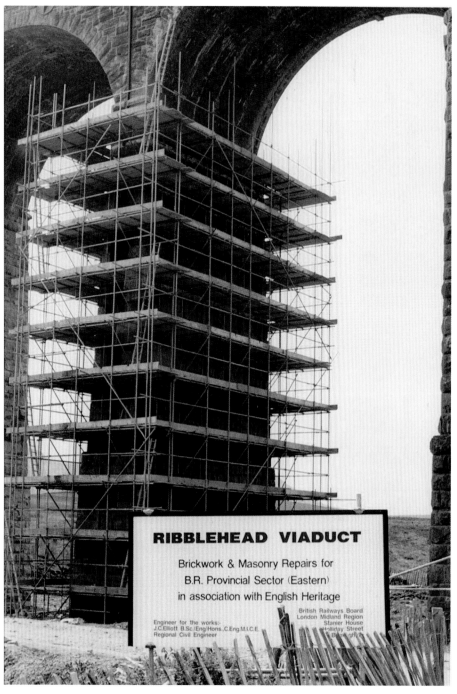

RIBBLEHEAD VIADUCT

Brickwork & Masonry Repairs for
B.R. Provincial Sector (Eastern)
in association with English Heritage

Engineer for the works:-
J.C.Elliott B.Sc.(Eng)Hons.,C.Eng.M.I.C.E.
Regional Civil Engineer

British Railways Board
London Midland Region
Stanier House
Holliday Street
Birmingham

Ribblehead viaduct was at the centre of British Rail's attempts to close the line in 1985. They argued that the viaduct was falling down and that its replacement or re-building cost far out-weighed the rundown railway. Set at £6 million, BR was asked by the Ministry of Transport in 1989 to do a series of tests on the centre pier and arch to assess the problem. Rain was the main problem. Water was infiltrating from the top of the viaduct through to the inside of the stonework of the piers and in winter, frost and ice caused the stone to crack.

The problem became the focal point for not only the authorities but for supporters trying to keep the line open. Other estimates for repairs to the viaduct came to £2 million and so the fight was on to find a solution.

After the government instructed BR to keep the line open in April 1989, a programme of repairs started by closing the line in the autumn and taking up all the old track and ballast from the viaduct. A new waterproof membrane was fitted and other repairs carried out.
As a BR advertisement put it, "Re-opening shortly. For a long, long time".

But it was in the summer of 1990 that the main works to restore the structure began. Structural Engineer, Tony Freschini, who had been in charge of earlier repairs, became the Resident Engineer of the project over a two year period.

Scaffolding appeared around most of the 24 arches and piers and work started. Cracked stonework was either repaired or in the worst cases, replaced by a concrete block using a fibreglass mould to make the outer facing side look like the original.

The final cost of £3 million, half the original BR estimate, was found by English Heritage, Settle-Carlisle Railway Trust, Railway Heritage Trust, the Rural Development Commission and BR themselves.

Epilogue

Books have been written about the decline and glorious re-birth of the Settle-Carlisle railway. Briefly, the line was allowed to decline and waste away for decades. Expresses ceased to run. Goods traffic was diverted to other routes or withdrawn. In 1985, British Rail announced its intention to close the line. Those who objected set about gathering economic facts. The main pressure group was the Friends of the Settle-Carlisle Line. Its membership rose to well over 3,000. The strength of the opposition to line closure exceeded 22,000.

A public inquiry was held, then another. The Minister seemed unmoved. The line would be closed. The government attempted to privatise the Settle-Carlisle, a phase that was enacted in the 1980s, when "steam specials" became popular and passenger figures rose steeply. On Tuesday, April 11th 1989, Mr Channon, the Transport Minister, rose in Parliament to reply to a question posed by the Member for Skipton Division. He startled BR and delighted objectors when he refused consent to close the line.

The 1990s was a period of improvement along the line. Many stations had their platforms raised and in the case of here at Dent, extended to cater for longer trains. Modern Sprinter units now form the main service from Leeds through to Carlisle.

Roger Hardingham

With the great backlog of maintenance along the whole line, not only the viaducts required renovation. Most of the stations closed in 1970 were re-opened in 1986 and there followed a programme of repairs to such things as waiting shelters.

Top: The 'down' side shelter at Horton-in-Ribblesdale was completely restored to its former glory using a partnership of funding from local and national organisations. The Friends of the Settle-Carlisle Line were heavily involved in these projects and often led the way in the improvements.

Above left: The Friends also adopted many stations and as here at Dent were able to improve the overall look of them by putting in flower beds and creating signs. Note some of the old snow fences still in place. One of the new heritage lamps is also on view. Many stations now have these fitted, albeit powered by electricity these days.

Above right: A brand new waiting shelter was built for the station 'up' platform at Langwathby. It followed a design once associated at other stations on the line and so was in-keeping with traditional design. All, Roger Hardingham

The station at Settle in better times. With new platforms and a renovated station building, an addition was made in the form of the footbridge. Together with Kirkby Stephen, these bridges were put in to make it safer to cross the line.

So the Settle-Carlisle survives. An amazing turn-around for a line that nearly died. Ribblehead viaduct was renovated at a cost of £3m – which was about the sum not far short of that expended on the construction of the whole line. Settle Junction marked the point where, in the words of the late Eric Treacy, the Railway Bishop, the fireman's efforts with the shovel turn from little and often to more and often. Diesel-units sustain an adequate passenger service and a large number of freight trains are diesel-hauled, yet occasionally the staccato bark of a steam locomotive on the Drag is heard. A "steam special" is due.

To many, wrote Geoff Bounds, Project Manager on the Settle-Carlisle, the sight of steam feels right – a combination of raw power in an area of rugged natural beauty. Man and machine blend their efforts to overcome the demands of moving a heavy train over the roof of England and battling against the often fierce elements that are so much a part of that area."

John Watson, a former MP for Skipton District, who with other MPs supported the movement for the retention of the line when it seemed it might be closed, summed up its significance in a moving way.

Above: **With a renewed interest in the line, freight trains also started to appear again over the route. The first trains were from Drax power station in Yorkshire in 1994 which produced a large amount of gypsum. This by-product is taken out by rail to Kirkby Thore where a large factory producing plaster products is based. In this view a train of empty coal wagons works north and would eventually arrive in Scotland to be refilled.** Roger Hardingham

Right: **Since the line was reprieved in April 1989, millions of pounds has been spent on upgrading work. Since the late 1990s nearly £100m has been spent by Network Rail on track relaying. Most of the whole railway between Settle and Carlisle has been replaced which has required the digging out and removal of thousands of tons of ballast and bringing in new sections of track which now form continuous welded lengths.** Roger Hardingham

Opposite page: **One of the major tasks in the renovation of Ribblehead viaduct was the excavation of the old track and ballast and the fitting of a new waterproof membrane. The former double track here was reduced to just a single line which is how it remains today.** BR

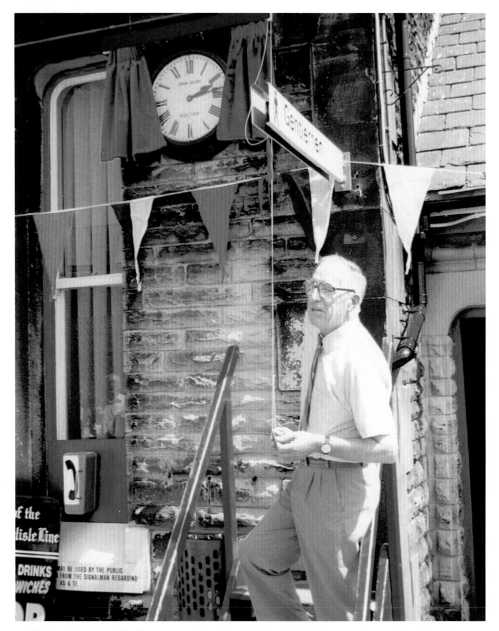

The author unveils the restored station clock at Settle in 1997. Several stations have since had their clocks restored thanks to the Friends of the Settle-Carlisle Line.